A Long Love Letter

MARGARET RUTH BAKER

Mall Publishing Co.

THE PRINTED WORD THE PLANTED SEED

HIGHLAND PARK, ILLINOIS

A LONG LOVE LETTER by Margaret Ruth Baker

Published by
Mall Publishing Co.
641 Homewood Avenue
Highland Park, IL 60035
www.mallpublishing.biz
Toll Free: 877-203-2453

Scripture references are the author's paraphrase.

Cover art: Tree of Life tapestry by Becky Patterson

Cover and text revised by Marlon Villadiego

International Standard Book Number: 1-934165-15-8

07 08 09 --- 8 7 6 5 4 3 2
Printed in the United States of America

For licensing / copyright information, for additional copies or for use in specialized settings contact:

WORD MINISTRIES
P.O. Box 367
Bulverde, Texas 78163
Phone: 830-980-3088
Email: info@mallpublishing.biz

Contents

Introduction

This is a book that has been written on my knees. I do not take lightly the awesome responsibility of touching God's holy Word. I remember with reverent awe the stern warnings in the Book of Revelation: *If anyone adds to the Book, God will add to that one the plagues in the Book and if anyone takes away from the Book, the Lord will take away from them their part in the Holy City and their name from the Book of Life.*

I am so very grateful for the scribes who devoted their lives to scrupulously copying the Word of God. I am so thankful for the discovery of the Dead Sea Scrolls and for their proof of the accuracy of God's Word. It is not my intention to change Scripture in any way, but simply to restate and amplify God's Word. As far as I know, I have used every major reputable English translation of the Bible. If there are any that I have missed, I want to quickly acquire them and continue my search. I have not directly quoted from any one translation; instead, I have offered a new rendition, drawn from the many so that you will have gift upon gift, blessing upon blessing and love upon love from your beloved Bridegroom, the Lord of lords and the King of kings. Jesus is the Word of God, and He loves you.

I feel that our merciful Lord is smiling on this work. It was a labor of love. I feel especially privileged to have been able to spend so much time in the Word. The Lord gave me that time, and now, my gift to you is the fruit of that time. This is the best gift I can think of to share with you, dear Reader.

I have not even scratched the surface. There is such endless treasure yet to be found! I invite you to share my joy and continue the search. You will find nuggets of pure gold and priceless jewels of the Kingdom. Every word of Scripture is so precious and beautiful and meaningful.

Even though I got to read this love letter first, I knew, all the while, that it was to be passed through me to you—A LONG LOVE LETTER addressed to you. I hope and pray that as you read this book, you will be able to know and deeply experience, say and sing from your heart, "Jesus loves me, this I know, for the Bible tells me so!"

Chapter 1

Proposal

 CALL

Yes, Dear One, you are called out of the world and into communion with Me. You are called by Me for My purpose and plan and it is a noble, honorable, fulfilling call and plan. Rejoice that you are one of the Called Ones. You are called with an irrevocable call. I will never change My mind or withdraw the call. You can rest in the fact that you are called forever, eternally without end.

You have answered the call with joy at being chosen. You have dropped everything to answer the call. You have gladly turned from the world to Me. Therefore, when you call I will answer. I will be right there, day and night, at your beck and call. When you call to Me, I will show you great and mighty things, which you know not.

My call, to come and follow Me, is really a love song sung to My Beloved. It is the rejoicing of My heart when the answer is, Yes. My proposal, to My Loved Ones, is continually going out. Let all who hear it say, Yes and come and follow Me.

Jeremiah 31:3

I have loved you with an everlasting love. My love for you is an eternal love that will last forever. I have dearly loved you from of old. I have always loved you. I have never quit loving you. That is why I have been so patient and kind. You are precious to Me. In grace, have I called you. With mercy and compassion, I have drawn you and made you come to Me. I maintain My faithful love and My unfailing care for you and I will continue to show you My faithfulness and lovingkindness. I love you and I draw you gently home. Expect love, more love and still more love!

1 Peter 2:9

You are the ones chosen by God for the high calling of priestly work. You are chosen to be a holy people—God's instruments to do His work. You are a chosen generation, a royal priesthood, a kingdom of priests, ministers of the Kingdom, a holy nation, a consecrated and dedicated people, God's special, peculiar treasure. God, Himself, has chosen you. You are God's elect. You are people claimed by God for His Own, the people, who belong to God. You are God's very own purchased and redeemed ones. You are called to tell of the night and day difference He has made in you—from nothing to something, from rejected to accepted. You are called to praise God—to sing His praise and to set forth His praises. You are entrusted with the proclamation of the goodness of God. You were chosen to tell about the excellent qualities of God. You are called to make known and proclaim abroad His wondrous excellencies, to display the virtues, the perfections and the glorious works of the One, Who called you out of darkness into His amazingly wonderful, marvelous light!

Romans 11:29

God's free gifts and His call are irrevocable. He never withdraws them when once they are given. He does not change His mind about those to whom He gives His grace or to whom He sends His call. God never takes back the gifts He has given or forgets about the people He has chosen. There is no such thing as God coming to regret the gracious gifts He bestows or the call He sends out. God's gifts and call are under full warranty, never canceled, never rescinded. God never changes His mind about the people He calls or the blessings He gives them.

Jeremiah 33:2–3

The Lord, Who made you and formed you and established you, the Lord, Who made the earth, the One, Who formed the earth and set it in place and established it, says, Call unto Me and I will answer you and show you great and mighty things. I will reveal hidden things, which you do not know, great beyond your reach of knowledge. Call to Me and I will tell you wondrous things. I will share with you important and remarkable secrets that you have never known or heard before.

1 Thessalonians 5:24

Faithful is He, Who is calling you to Himself. Utterly trustworthy is He. If He said it—He will do it! He will fulfill His call by hallowing you and keeping you. He will complete His work. He will finish what He set out to do. Completely dependable is He, Who gives you the Divine summons unto salvation and He will bring it to pass. He will accomplish it. He will keep His Word. He is true to His Word. God, Who called you, will do this for you just as He promised. He will not fail you.

Isaiah 45:2–3

I will open doors for you. City gates will not stop you. I will precede you and make the crooked places straight, the rough places smooth and the rugged places plain. I will march before you and flatten the hills that loom up. I will go before you, leveling the mountains. I will go ahead of you, clearing and paving the road. I, Myself, will prepare your way.

I will break in pieces the doors of brass and cut asunder the bars of iron. I will smash and breakdown city gates of bronze. I will snap and shatter barred entrances. No gates will be barred to you. I will open gateways before you so that your gates will be closed no more.

I will lead you to buried treasure, secret caches of valuables. I will hand over to you hidden riches in secret places. I will give you hoarded wealth from dark vaults that you may know that it is I, Jehovah, the Lord, the God of Israel, Who calls you by your name. Yahweh, the One, Who calls you by your name, is calling you.

Isaiah 51:15–16

I AM the Lord, your God, Who can stir up the sea to storm, causing its waves to roar and thunder and by rebuke, I restrain it and its waves are calm. I AM the Lord, your Maker—the Lord Almighty. I AM Yahweh. I AM Adonai, your God. I AM Saboath, the Lord of Armies and the God of Angel Armies. The Lord of Hosts is My name. I AM Jehovah. I AM the Eternal. I AM the Lord All-Powerful by name.

I have unfurled and stretched out the heavens. I have fixed the heavens as a tabernacle. I have set all the stars in space. I have laid the foundation of the earth. Setting it on a solid foundation, I have established the earth.

I have given you My teaching. I will teach you how to talk,

word by word. I have put My words in your mouth and on your lips. I will give you the words I want you to say.

I, personally, watch over you. I will keep you safe in the palm of My hand. I have hidden you safely within My hand. I have shielded you and sheltered you with My hand. I have covered you with the shadow of My hand. I will cover you with My hands and protect you.

I AM the One, Who says, You are Mine! Welcome, My people!

 LISTEN

Precious Love—I am grateful for your spiritual ears that listen attentively for My voice. Thank you, for being attuned to My Spirit and for needing the quiet as you need your necessary sustenance so that you can listen to the still, small voice within. You will become more and more sensitive to My voice and have no trouble hearing as you draw closer to your Beloved. You will come close, to listen to My whispers of love and appreciation and encouragement.

Thank you, for cherishing this time of quiet, alone, with your Loved One. I appreciate your spiritual ears that are eager to hear. I encourage you to listen as I share My heart—first with you and then with a multitude, who will listen.

Matthew 11:15

Are you listening to Me? If you are willing to listen, listen now. Really listen and heed carefully what you hear. Pay attention and consider, perceive and comprehend. Listen and hear!

Revelation 3:20

Behold! Here I AM! I stand at the door and knock. I AM always standing there knocking. If anyone listens to My voice and hears and heeds and opens the door—I will come in. We will share together as friends. We will feast together!

Revelation 22:17

Both the Holy Spirit and the Bride say, Come! Whoever listens and hears the invitation, must answer, Come! Let everyone who is listening say, Come!

Let everyone who is thirsty come! Let all who are painfully conscious of their need of those things by which the soul is refreshed, supported and strengthened, all who earnestly desire it, let them come and drink freely from the gift of life-giving water, the Water of Life.

Matthew 7:24–25

Anyone, who comes to Me and continues to listen to My words and practice their teachings and acts upon them, obeying them, will be like a sensible, prudent, practical, wise man who dug and went down deep and laid the foundation of his house upon bed-rock. The house was so well constructed that when the rain fell and the rivers overflowed, when the torrent broke loose and the floods came, when the winds blew and howled and beat against that house, it was not shaken. It did not fall because it was well built, founded securely on the rock. The words I speak to you are foundational words—words to build your life on.

James 1:21–22, 25

Let our Gardener, God, landscape you with the Word, making a salvation garden. Receive, with meekness, the engrafted Word.

With a humble spirit, take in the Message, which is planted in your heart. Welcome the Word which, when implanted and rooted in your heart, contains the power to save your soul.

Be doers of the Word, obey the message and do not be merely listeners of it. Remember it is a message to be obeyed not just listened to. Put the message into practice. Act on the Word. Find delight and affirmation in action. Don't just listen to it, betraying yourselves into deception by reasoning contrary to the truth. God will bless you for doing it.

The person, who continually studies God's perfect teachings that make people free and who remains committed to those teachings, will be blessed. People like that don't merely listen and forget, they actually do what God's teachings say. Anyone who listens and looks carefully and steadily into the faultless law of freedom, the flawless law of liberty and is faithful to it—that one will be happy in the very act and deed and practice of obedience. The, truly, happy people make a habit of doing what the Word says. They live and abide in its company.

God will bless you in everything you do if you will listen and obey and not hear and forget.

Jeremiah 29:12–13

When you call to Me, when you come and pray to Me, I will listen to you. When you search for Me with all of your heart, you will find Me. If you seek and look for Me, in earnest, I will make sure you are not disappointed. When you want it more than anything else, I will reveal Myself to you. When you require Me as a vital necessity, I will be at hand, I will be near. I will be with you. I will be there.

 ALWAYS

Beloved—I see and hear and listen to you just as you wait expectantly listening for My voice. My Beloved hear My voice and another voice they will not follow. Be not concerned. I won't let you even listen to the wrong voice and I surely won't allow you to follow after the wrong shepherd. You can rest, truly rest, in the knowledge that I will never leave you or forsake you. I AM with you always, in all ways. I will even minister to you as you rest at night so that there will be no time lost. This will be a quick work.

As you take and send My Word, you also will personally deliver this love letter to bless My beloved Bride. I AM even now preparing hearts to receive, with joy, a love letter written especially for them. They are expectantly waiting for a personal message, of love, from Me. I will fulfill the longing of their hearts with A Long Love Letter written from My heart to theirs.

Beloved, you see why I have chosen you! You count everything else as loss to be with your Beloved. Thank you, for preferring My constant abiding Presence over anything the world has to offer. Your yielded spirit allows Me to have deep and personal communication with you. Your spiritual ears, ever listening for My voice over all other sounds, allow Me to speak to you alone. I will be with you wherever you are. I will be guiding and directing and using your yielded spirit to reach out to others. I will comfort them and minister love to them through you. I will show them that I love them and care for them through your yielded spirit. I have promised My abiding Presence,

day and night, on all occasions, at all times, in all ways,
always. I will never leave you or forsake you—I promise.

John 10:27

I AM the Good Shepherd and I know and recognize those that are My Own and My Own know and recognize Me. The sheep that are My Own, hear and listen to and respond to My voice. I know them and they follow Me and another's voice they will not follow. The sheep that are Mine are always listening for My voice. They are in the habit of listening to My voice. I know them by experience. They take the same road that I take.

Matthew 18:20

Remember, I AM with you always, day after day after day, perpetually, uniformly, on every occasion. Yes, know that I will be with you for all time, to the very close and conclusion of the age, to the end of the world, to the very end of time.

Hebrews 13:5–6

God has told us and the statement is recorded. God, Himself, says, I will not! I will in no way, fail you or leave you without support or give you up. I will never let go of you. I will never, never abandon you or walk off and leave you or desert you. I will not, I will not, I will not in any degree leave you helpless or let you down or relax My hold on you. I will never let go of My grip on you. No indeed! Assuredly not!

I will always sustain you and uphold you. I will never forget you. I will never leave you or forsake you.

Since this is true, we can meet life fearlessly. We take comfort and are encouraged. The Lord has promised that He will not leave us or desert us. That makes us feel like saying with courage and confidence—we can boldly claim and fearlessly say, without doubt, The Lord is My Helper, I will not fear or dread or be terrified! What can anyone do to me?

I am fearless, no matter what happens! Who or what can get to me? God is there ready to help. Since God has promised and assured me that He is on my side, why should I be afraid? I fear nothing! What can mere mortals do to me? The Lord is my Champion and hastens to my cry. I will not be put in fear of anyone or anything. The Lord helps me!

Joshua 1:5

I will always be with you and help you. Just as I was with Moses so shall I be with you. I will not fail you or forsake you. I will never neglect you or abandon you or desert you. I will not take My help from you.

Be strong and of good courage. Be resolute. Be firm and steadfast. Take heart and be brave. No one will be able to oppose or resist you, successfully, as long as you live. No one will be able to stand before you or defeat you, all the days of your life.

Isaiah 42:16

I will not leave My people. I will make the place that was dark before them, to be light. I will smooth and straighten out the road ahead of them. I will make their rugged and rough and rocky places into level ground. I will turn quagmires into solid ground. I will make their crooked way and their twisted roads, plain and straight before them. These are the things I will do. I will not forsake them. I promise, I will not leave them forsaken.

I will lead them along a way they never knew. I will guide them

10

on paths they have never traveled. Their road may be dark and rough but I will give them light. I will keep them from stumbling. This is My solemn promise, I will not abandon them. I will not neglect My people. These things, I will do without fail. Yes, I will, indeed, do these things. These are promises I will keep. These things I AM determined to do for them. I will not leave them undone.

Psalm 139:7–12

Where could I go from Your Spirit? I can never escape Your Spirit. Where can I flee from Your Presence? I can never get away from Your Presence. Where can I run to get away from You? If I ascend up to Heaven, You are there. If I sink into the nether world and if I make my bed in Sheol, the place of the dead—Behold! You are there! If I take the wings of the dawn and come to rest on the western horizon, already You are there waiting for me. If I climb on the rays of the morning sun and land on the most distant shores of the sea, where the sun sets, there Your powerful arm would guide me and protect me. If I dwell in the uttermost parts, the furtherest limits of the sea, even there, Your strength would support me and Your hand would hold me fast. If I say, Surely the darkness shall cover me and the night will hide me in its curtains. The dark is not dark to You. The night is as bright as the day to You. The darkness and the light are both alike to You.

I can never be lost from my God!

Psalm 125:2

As the mountains are round about Jerusalem, so the Lord is round about His people from this time forth and forevermore. God encircles His people. He always has and He always will.

Isaiah 49:15–16

Can a loving mother forget her nursing child? Does a woman not have compassion or fail to cherish the child of her womb? Can she feel no love for the child she has borne? Can a mother feel no kindness or pity for the infant, who came from her own body? Although mothers may forget, I will not forget you. Yes, if even these were to forget, I can never forget you. You are always in My thoughts. Behold, I have engraved you upon the palms of My hands. I have indelibly imprinted your name on My hands. See, a picture of you is on the palm of each of My hands. I have portrayed you on My hands. Your portrait is always before Me.

Psalm 16:8–9

I have set the Lord, always, before me. I keep the Eternal before me at all times. Because He is at my right hand, I shall not be moved. He makes me to stand firm. I will not stumble. I shall not be overthrown. Nothing can shake me. I cannot be disturbed for He is right beside me. I am always aware of the Lord's Presence. He is always near. I keep the Eternal within my sight always. I keep Him, continually, on my mind. With Him so close, I cannot fail.

No wonder my heart is glad and My inner self rejoices! My whole being is filled with joy and exults. My body, also, shall rest without a care and dwell confidently in safety. My flesh shall abide secure in hope. I am so thankful! I feel completely secure. I know the Lord is always with me.

I will always look to You, Lord, as You stand beside me and protect me from all fear. With all of my heart, I will celebrate! I can safely rest and settle down secure.

GRACE

Yes, Loved One, I AM here and I hear. If you could see with My eyes, you would see that you are right now, not at some future day, walking in divine health. You are right this very minute beautiful, lovely and full of grace. You are "grace full." I can't pour down any more grace than you already have and are walking in right now. My grace is an equal measure of My love and that is unlimited, without measure, eternally and unconditionally yours.

Your grace full walk will lead many into the Kingdom. They will see your amazing grace and My favor and blessing and they will turn from darkness to light, seeking that same measure of grace, favor and blessing. I have chosen you to lead by example of grace. Therefore, you need never even ask for grace, it is now yours in full measure. I have filled you full to overflowing with an abundant, everlasting supply.

Grace is not yours to give away. You can't even share your supply of grace with others. It comes only from Me and it is My decision and My choice. You can only share by showing others the beauty of grace—the grace I have so willingly and joyfully given, without measure, to you—My beautiful, gracious, grace full Chosen One.

Isaiah 30:18

The Lord is patiently waiting for you to come to Him so that He can show you how kind He is. The Lord earnestly waits, expecting, looking and longing to be gracious to you. He wants to comfort you and deal kindly with you. The Lord is waiting to show you His love, His lovingkindness, His compassion and His mercy. He will arise to pardon you. The Eternal longs to favor you and show you His grace. He will conquer you to bless you, just as He said, for the Lord is faithful to all His promises. The Lord is a faithful God, a God of fair judgment and a God of justice. The Lord always does what is right. God takes the time to do everything right. Everything!

Blessed, happy, fortunate, to be envied are all those, who earnestly wait for the Lord—all those, who expectantly look for Him and long for Him. All those, who hope for His favor, His victory, His peace, His joy, His love and His matchless, unbroken companionship, will be happy. He blesses all those, who trust in Him.

Hebrews 4:16

Let us fearlessly, with assurance and with the fullest confidence, draw near to our gracious God. Let us come, boldly, to the throne of grace, the throne of God's unlimited, unmerited favor that we may receive mercy for our failures. There, we will find grace to help for every need—appropriate help, well-timed help, coming just when we need it. We will find God's spiritual strength in our hour of need.

Let us be brave and come to God's throne where there is grace, freely, flowing. There we will find mercy and grace to help us in every situation.

2 Corinthians 6:1

As God's partners, God's collaborators, as cooperators with God, we labor together with Him. Sharing in God's work as fellow workers, we beg you not to receive the grace of God in vain. His grace is the merciful kindness by which He exerts His holy influence on souls and turns them to Christ, keeping and strengthening them. As God's co-workers, we appeal to you, we beseech you, do not receive God's grace to no purpose. Do not fail to use the grace of God. Don't reject the message of God's great kindness. Make good use of God's kindness to you. Don't squander, one bit of, the marvelous life God has given you. We entreat you, don't let God's love poured out upon you, receive an ineffectual welcome or be wasted.

Ephesians 2:4–5

It is because of His great love for us that God is so rich in mercy and abundant compassion. He has loved us with a wonderful, intense and incredible love. With what an excess of love, He has loved us! We are saved by His grace, His unmerited favor and not by our achieving it. God's wonderful kindness rescued us when we were dead—slain by our own sins and offenses, our transgressions and trespasses, our faults and shortcomings. With immense mercy, by His lovingkindness, He has quickened us. He has raised us up and made us alive together in fellowship and union with Christ. He has made us live again and called us to share the life of Christ. He has given us the very life of Christ, Himself! He has given us the same new life with which He quickened Him. For it is by His grace, His favor, His mercy and His great love, which we did not deserve, that we are saved and delivered from judgment and made partakers of Christ's salvation.

Colossians 1:6

The Word of God is bearing fruit and still growing by its own inherent power. The Good News is increasing and spreading throughout the entire world. Everywhere it bears fruit, just as it has reached you and remains with you. It does not diminish or weaken with time but gets stronger and larger.

This same Gospel is changing lives everywhere just as it changed yours when you heard about and understood God's great kindness and grace. You came to know grace, the undeserved favor of God, in reality—deeply, clearly and thoroughly becoming accurately and intimately acquainted with it. You came to know experientially God's grace, His gracious intent and what His wonderful kindness, truly, means.

The Word of God is producing lovely lives, like yours, all over the world!

 PLAN

Beloved—It is a lost art to cherish peace and quiet and solitude and a set apart, holy life. That makes it even more precious to Me. So many fill their lives with the clutter of the mundane, the unimportant and the trivial that will all be burned up as wood, hay and stubble when they leave life and earth. They will look back and only see a puff of smoke, a vapor disappearing that represents all of their efforts and time on earth. They have not stopped long enough to search for My direction. They fail to look up and live, truly live, the purpose and meaning I have planned for their lives. They are caught up on a treadmill, in a maze that leads to nowhere, amid the noise of nothing.

Thank you, for coming, for listening and for waiting attentively for My direction and purpose for your life. Your taking time to come apart will be greatly rewarded. I will share My love and My concern and My interest in the plan I have for your life. Because of My great love for the unique creation I have made in you, it will be a way like

no other—one that fits only you. It will be a plan to bless
you, for your good and welfare, a plan to prosper you in
all areas and ways and means. Reach out and embrace My
perfect plan for your life. It will save you from much need-
less sorrow and pain and suffering and disappointment. As
you wait and watch and listen—I will share My heart with
you and bless you abundantly for I, truly, love and care
about you and long to commune with you.

Jeremiah 29:11

For I know the plans I have for you, declares the Lord. I AM
mindful of the plans I have made for your good, says Jehovah.
The thoughts I think toward you are of peace and wholeness
and not trouble or misfortune, says Adonai. I, alone, know My
purpose for you and it is for your well-being and to prosper you.
I will bless you with a future of success and not suffering. I AM
reserving a future full of hope for you. I have plans for your welfare and not for woe. I have given you a destiny and an expected
end, declares Yahweh.

Psalm 139:1–6

O Lord, You have searched and examined My heart thoroughly. You have looked deep into my heart, Lord and You know
all about me. You know when I sit and when I stand, when I am
resting or when I am working. You are acquainted and familiar
with all my ways. You notice everything I do and everywhere I go.
You chart the path ahead of me. Every moment You know where
I am. You tell me where to stop and rest.

When far away, You know my every thought. From Heaven,

You are aware of my thoughts when they are scarcely formed. You know what I'm going to say before I even say it. There is not a word on my tongue still unuttered but Behold! O Lord, You know it altogether!

You have shielded me with Your hand. You have provided for every possible situation. You sustain me by Your power. With Your powerful arm, You protect me from every side. You both proceed and follow me. You are all around me, in front of me and behind me. Your reassuring Presence is with me coming and going, when I leave and when I get back. I'm never out of Your sight. From beginning to end, You know me, O Lord, for You have formed me and placed Your hand of blessing on my head.

Such knowledge is beyond my grasp. It is so high I cannot reach it. It is amazing to me and more than I can understand or comprehend. It is a mystery I cannot fathom. Your plans for me are glorious—too wonderful to believe!

Proverbs 19:21

Many are the plans in the human heart—their hearts are full of schemes and designs and devices. People make all kinds of plans but only the Lord's plan will happen. It is the Eternal's purpose that prevails. It is Adonai's plan that is accomplished. The advice of the Lord will endure, the counsel of the Lord will stand firm. The plans of Yahweh will prevail and be established.

Proverbs 16:3

Commit to the Lord, all that you do and your plans will be fulfilled. Roll all of your works onto the Lord. Trust your plans, wholly, to Him and He will cause your thoughts to become agreeable to His will so that your plans and your thoughts will be established and achieved. Depend on the Lord in whatever you do and you will succeed. Commit your business to the Lord and your business will prosper. Entrust all your efforts to the Lord. Put God in charge and His plan will take place.

 PURPOSE

Yes, My Chosen One, I have chosen you, long ago, to write down and to deliver My love letter to My beloved Bride. You were chosen for a purpose and I have set you apart for My plan. I have given your life purpose and meaning for My purpose. Out of the whole earth, I have chosen you. Rejoice and be exceedingly glad! My purpose is to bless you, not condemn you. My plan is to release you from any burden of sin. My plan is to give you life and life abundant—a rich, free, victorious life. My purpose is to bless you and show My love for you in countless ways—to tell you of My love and even send messengers to tell you of My love for you. You will come to deeply believe and know, without a shadow of doubt, that I love you. I have given you life and life abundant to fulfill My purpose in the earth.

Beloved Bride, I promise that you will learn and grow and change as never before. This may seem like the most quiet, peaceful time of your life, this holy solitary confinement with your Beloved but it will be a time when so much is accomplished in every area, in all directions, in all ways, by all means. Everything will be made new, in this time of inner and outer growth. You will not look to another or in any other direction. You will not listen to another voice or the sounds of the earth. Rejoice! And again I say, Rejoice with Me! Be glad, exceedingly glad and full of joy! You are chosen and cherished and especially treasured. I have chosen you for My purpose, My beloved Bride.

Romans 8:28

Those, who love God, have His aid and help and interest in everything. All things are fitting into the fulfillment of His design and resulting in good for those He has called for His plan and purpose.

He will use even tough, hard times to bring about good in your life. We know that God is always at work for the good of everyone who loves Him. They are the ones God has chosen for His plan and purpose.

For those, who love God and keep on loving Him, God causes all things continually, everything that happens, to fit together into a pattern, for their good, for those called according to His purpose.

Psalm 138:8

Your steadfast love, O Lord, endures and continues forever. Your mercy and Your lovingkindness are eternal. Do not abandon or forsake the works of Your Own hands. Don't quit or give up on me or leave me now. Don't leave Your work unfinished.

The Lord will fulfill His purpose for me. The Lord will perfect that which concerns me. The Lord will complete His purpose for my life.

Proposal

Psalm 57:1–3

Be good to me and show me Your favor. Be merciful and gracious to me, O God. I look to You for protection. I run to You for safety. My soul trusts in You. I find shelter and confidence in You. My soul hides in You. Yes, in the shadow of Your wings, I will take refuge until the storms have past, until the deadly danger dies down.

I pray to You, my Protector. I will call unto my accomplishing God, Who has ever befriended me, to the Most High God, Who fulfills His purpose for me. I cry to the God Most High, Who performs His purposes for me and will surely complete them!

He will reach down from Heaven and deliver me. He will send down His steadfast love. He will send from Heaven and save me. He will send forth His lovingkindness, His grace, His truth and His faithfulness. God will demonstrate His loving mercy and show forth His love that never fails.

 THE WAY

My Dearly Beloved—Don't look back to pain and sorrow and shame and suffering. Whatsoever things are lovely—whatsoever things are of good report—whatsoever things are true and good and honorable—those things that are right and righteous—think on these things. Dwell on these things and you will have happy memories. You will enjoy looking back and you will be grateful for all of My many blessings raining down upon you. You will see that you were protected and cherished and loved beyond words. I will show you the good, the better and the best along the way. I will hold your hand and lead you back through your life and you will see that you were special.

You were chosen and prepared for such a time as this. The days of preparation were necessary for this day.

I will see that you have My mind, My thoughts, My understanding and My wisdom in every situation. Part of the perfect peace, I have promised, is a mind at rest. I promise, a mind not grasping hold of ideas and trying to figure things out, not wondering about the multiple choices and struggling to find the right choice among the many. I promise a peaceful, yielded mind—yielded to the Master Mind. I will renew your mind. I will give you a mind that is, truly, at rest—waiting for the wisdom of the ages and trusting in the perfect peace, of perfect trust and faith.

I will lift the burden of having to make the right decisions and choices from you. In leading and guiding you constantly, I will always help you to make the right choice. You can relax and rest and receive, knowing that I have taken from you the striving and straining and all of the hard work. I have removed the heavy responsibility, of weighing every situation. I have removed from you the labor of sifting through the facts and trying to figure it all out and make the right decision over large and small things, over any and all things, over every possible choice. You will know, with blessed assurance, the right choice to choose. I will be right there in every situation, every part and parcel of your life saying, "This is the way, walk in it."

The way to perfect peace is a mind at rest. A renewed mind is a gift of My love for you and My tender loving care.

Philippians 4:8

If you value the approval of God, fill your mind with those things that are good. Your thoughts must continually dwell on whatever is worthy of reverence. Don't ever stop thinking about what is holy and worthy of praise. Think about all that you can praise God for and be glad about. Think about what is, truly, worthwhile. Fix your thoughts on all that commands respect and on any moral excellence. Let your mind be filled with whatsoever things are true, all that rings true and is of good report.

Think about all of the fine and good things in others—whatever is lovely and lovable, endearing, friendly, amiable, gracious and pleasing. Think about whatever is kind and winsome and admirable. Think about whatever is honorable, honest and dignified. Think about whatever is lofty, high toned, upright and righteous.

Focus your thoughts on what is commendable, acceptable and fair, what is pure and proper. If there be any virtue, if there is any excellence, anything that is beautiful and respected—think on and weigh and take into account these things to be your treasures. Cherish the thought of these things. Make them the subject of your careful reflection. Fill your mind with and meditate on these things.

Romans 12:2

Don't imitate the ways of the world. Don't let the world around you squeeze you into its mold. Don't become well-adjusted to your culture or adapted to its customs and behavior. Be a new and different person with a fresh newness in all you do and think. Learn how God's ways will really satisfy you. Embrace what God has for you. God brings out the best and develops well-formed maturity in you. Let God remold your mind. Let Him change the way you think. Be transformed by the complete change that has come over your mind—the renewing of your mind. Recognize what God wants and quickly respond. Find and follow God's way and His will for you so that all you do is well pleasing and good and acceptable to Him.

Proverbs 3:5

Trust in the Lord with all your heart. Lean not to your own understanding. Don't depend on your own judgment or insight. Put no faith in your own perception. Don't try to figure everything out on your own.

Always let the Lord lead. Seek His will in all you do. Listen for God's voice in everything you do and everywhere you go. In all your ways, acknowledge Him, rely on Him, lean on Him and be confident in the Lord. Remember the Lord in all you do and He will direct your path and give you success. He will clear the road and level and smooth your path. He will make a straight way for you to follow.

Isaiah 30:20–21

The Lord will be with you to teach you. You will see the Lord, your Teacher and He will guide you. Your Teacher will never hide Himself or leave you anymore but your eyes will constantly behold your Teacher. Your eyes will watch your Guide and whenever you deviate to the right or to the left, your ears will heed the command, "This is the road, now follow it. This is the way, stay on it." If you go the wrong way, your ears will hear a voice saying, "Turn around and walk here. You should walk this way. Do not turn aside." When you might go right or left, you will hear a whisper behind you saying "This is the way, walk in it."

Isaiah 48:17

This is what the Lord, your Redeemer, the Holy One of Israel says, I AM the Lord your God, Who teaches you what is best for you, Who directs you in the way you should go.

This is the Word of the Eternal, your Deliverer, I AM the Lord, your God, Who trains you and leads you along the path you should follow. I AM teaching you to be wise. I AM teaching you to profit.

Psalm 32:8

I will be your teacher. I will instruct you and I will guide you along the best pathway for your life. I will advise you and watch over you with My eye upon you. I will counsel you and watch your progress, says the Lord.

Psalm 18:30

The way of the Lord is a blameless and undefiled way. The ways of the Lord are without fault. How perfect in every way! All His promises prove true. The word of the Lord is tested and tried by fire. The words of the Lord are pure words.

He is a Defender and a Protector. He is a Shield to all those, who run to Him for help. For all, who take refuge and put their trust in Him and look to Him for protection, He is a sure Defense.

Exodus 15:13

In Your unfailing love, You will lead Your people. Lovingly, You lead the people You have saved. The people You rescue and redeem are led by Your merciful and powerful love to Your holy place. In Your power and strength and protection, You will guide them to Your holy dwelling. Your strong arms will carry them to the home of Your holiness, Your holy habitation.

Proverbs 4:18

The path, of the uncompromisingly righteous, is like the light of dawn that shines more and more, ever brighter and clearer. It grows in brilliance until it reaches full strength and glory in the broad daylight of a perfect day. The ways of right-living people glow with light—the longer they live, the brighter they shine!

Psalm 25:8–10

Good and upright is the Lord. He is glad to teach the proper path to all, who go astray. He corrects the misdirected and sends them in the right direction. He guides sinners and wronged-ones to be righted. For the oppressed ones, He reveals His plans and makes His way clear. He is the essence of mercy and truth. He will teach the ways that are right and best for all those, who humbly turn to Him.

All of the paths of the Lord are grace and mercy and steadfast love. When we obey Him and cling to His promises and written instructions, every path He guides us on is fragrant with His lovingkindness, His truth and His faithfulness. All of the ways of the Lord are loving and sure. The Lord leads with unfailing love and faithfulness.

Proverbs 2:6–10

The Lord grants and supplies skillful and Godly wisdom! His every word is a treasure of knowledge and understanding. He grants good sense to His righteous ones. He is their shield, protecting them and guarding their pathway. He shows how to distinguish right from wrong, how to find the right decision every time. He stores up sound wisdom for the upright. He preserves the way of His Saints. He watches over everyone, who is faithful to Him.

You will understand what is just and fair in every course of life. Understanding will guard you and wisdom will save you. Truth will come into your heart and enter into the very center of your being, filling your life with joy.

Isaiah 58:11

The Lord will guide you always. He will continually satisfy you, in drought. He will refresh you, in dry places. He will slake your thirst, in parched lands. He will satisfy your needs with good things, in shimmering heat. He will give you a full life in the emptiest of places. He will satisfy even the scorched regions of your own soul.

He will renew your strength. He will make you healthy. He will keep you strong and well. You will have firm muscles and strong bones. Yes, your very bones will be invigorated!

Evermore shall the Eternal guide you, guarding you without fail. He will refresh and renew you. He will lead you until you are like a well-watered garden. You will be like an ever-flowing spring—a stream that never runs dry. You will be like an oasis with a steadfast spring.

John 14:6

Jesus said, "I AM the Way. I AM the Truth. I AM the Life, I alone, in contradistinction to all others. I, Myself, AM the road, the real, the true and the living way. Except through Me, no one can come into the Presence of the Father. The way to God, the Father, is through Me—the only way."

Chapter 2

I Will Provide for You

 GOOD EARTH

My Beloved Bride—See, how I delight in delighting you! In My great loving care for you, I will continually surprise you with My love. As you look around you, you will see manifest evidence of My love everywhere. Your thankful, grateful heart will open the channel of blessing even wider. Truly, the windows of heaven are open and pouring a continual rain of blessing upon you. Drink in the beauty and the wonder of My creation—it is My gift of love to you. I put the rainbow in the sky to surprise you and thrill you with My love. I have scattered wildflowers over the earth to delight you. Consider the beauty of My gift—even Solomon in all of his glory was not arrayed like one of these.

If you will look around you and look up and thank Me, you will see how very much I love you. You will know that I have, wondrously, created a breathtakingly beautiful home for you—in this good earth.

Because you have brought your First Fruits Offering with joy and you have willingly and joyfully given of your tithes and offerings that My house may be filled, I have rebuked the devourer for your sake. I will, surely, protect you from all evil and from the enemy who comes to steal, to rob and to kill. You need not be concerned. You will always be protected and provided for, with My loving care.

You will reap what others have sown for, truly, the wealth of the sinner is laid up for My Beloved. I give to My Beloved while they sleep and rest in Me. Rest and receive. Spread out your garments to catch the overflowing, abundant blessings that are on the way and even now are manifest all around you in the good earth. Blessings raining down on you are a gift of My love poured out on you so that you will know and experience My eternal, everlasting, enduring, abiding love for you.

Proverbs 3:9–10

Honor the Lord with your wealth, your money from righteous labor. Remember to thank the Lord with the first fruits of all of your income. Glorify God with the first and the best part of everything your land produces—then your barns will be filled with plenty and your storehouses will be full of more grain than you will ever need. Your vessels will overflow with the finest new wine.

Malachi 3:10–11

The Lord of Hosts says, Bring all the tithes, the whole one-tenth of your income, the entire full one-tenth of what you earn, into the storehouse that there may be food in My house and see if I will not open the windows of Heaven for you and pour you out a blessing. I will flood you with blessing after blessing—blessings until there is no more need, far beyond your needs—blessings so great you won't have room enough to take it in and contain it! The Lord All-Powerful says, I will open the floodgates of Heaven for you and pour down on you blessings without measure!

Try it! Try Me in this. Let Me prove it to you. Prove Me now by this, says the Lord. I AM the Lord your God and I challenge you to put Me to the test.

Your crops will be abundant for I will guard them from disease. I will rebuke the devourer for your sake. I will rebuke the devouring locust for you. I will forbid the locusts to destroy your crops. I will stop insects from eating and destroying the produce of your land, the yield of your soil. Your vine will not drop its fruit before its time. Nothing will stop your crops from producing. The Lord of Hosts, the Lord of Armies says, Your fields will not fail to bear!

Proverbs 13:22

The good bequeath an inheritance of moral stability and goodness to their children's children. A good life gets passed on to the grandchildren. Ill-gotten wealth ends up with good people. The sinner lays up treasure to enrich the good. The wealth of the wicked is laid up for the righteous. It has been stored up for and passed on to the godly. The wicked's wealth will find its way eventually into the hands of the righteous.

Psalm 127:2

It is in vain for you to rise up early and to take rest late—to eat the hard earned bread of wearisome, anxious toil. It is useless for you to work so hard, working your weary fingers to the bone, to earn a living. It is senseless to work hard for the food you eat, the bread of sorrows, since the Lord supplies the need of those He loves while they sleep. God takes care of His Own while they rest. God's blessings and gifts come to His loved ones as they sleep. God gives sleep to those He loves. God gives His beloved rest, for He wants His loved ones to have their proper rest. He enjoys giving sleep and rest to those He loves.

Luke 12:27–28

Walk out into the fields and look at the wildflowers. Have you ever seen color and design quite like that? If God gives such attention to wildflowers, most of them never even seen, don't you think He will do His best for you? Don't be preoccupied with getting—respond to God's giving. He wants to give you the very Kingdom itself!

Just look at and consider the lilies of the field and learn from them. They neither wearily work nor worry and yet Solomon with all of his riches, in his royal robes with his grandeur, splendor and magnificence, was never arrayed or so beautifully dressed as these. They are here today and gone tomorrow. How much more will He clothe and take care of you! God gives such beauty to everything that grows. He will surely do even more for you. How much more will He provide for you! Don't worry about your life—have faith.

Psalm 19:1–6

The heavens declare the glory of God. The firmament proclaims the wonder and the splendor of what His hands have made. The expanse of the sky shows forth what He has done, displaying His handiwork. Day after day pours forth speech and night after night breathes out knowledge. Day and night, they keep on revealing and telling about God. There is no speech or spoken word from the stars. Their voice is silent, no utterance at all, not a sound that anyone can hear. Yet, their message is in evidence. It travels around the world. The unspoken truth is spoken everywhere. Their good news has gone out through all the earth—their words to the end of the world. Their music goes through out all the earth.

In the heavens, the Lord has set a tabernacle for the sun. It arises from its covering horizon like a radiant bridegroom coming out of his chamber. From the horizon, it marches forth. It rejoices as a great runner—like a champion, who sees the track before him and is eager to run. Scorching deserts and melting ice, no one and no thing is hidden from the sun's heat.

God's Word vaults across the skies from sunrise to sunset warming hearts to faith.

Romans 1:20

Ever since the creation of the world, God's everlasting power and divinity have been known in and through the things He has made. The invisible qualities of God, those things that the eye is unable to see, have been made visible to the eye of reason. Even the mystery of the Godhead and His divine Being, His attributes and perfection are clearly perceptible and intelligible in His creation. They are easy to understand and can be studied by His works of creation. So everyone is altogether without any defense or justification. No one has any excuse, whatsoever, for not knowing God. To the end, they are without excuse! They can clearly see the earth, the sky and all of God's handiwork.

Open your eyes and there it is! Take a long thoughtful look at what God has created. Let your thoughts dwell on the works of His creation. All that is knowable about God lies plainly before our eyes. God, Himself, has made it plain for all to see.

Psalm 24:1

Look around you. Everything you see is God's—the heavens above and beyond, the whole earth is the Lord's and everything that is in it. The earth belongs to the Eternal and all earth holds, with all its wealth and all the people living in it, everything therein and the fullness thereof. The earth and everything good in it belongs to the Lord and is yours to enjoy.

1 Chronicles 16:30–34

Let the whole earth bow, in awe, before the Lord. Bow down before the Holy One! Tremble before His Presence, all the earth, for He has built the earth on immovable foundations. The Lord has steadied and settled the world. He has fixed the earth and set it firmly in place. The Lord put the earth in place and it is not moving! The Lord has established the earth firm and stable. It shall not be moved!

Let the heavens be glad and let the earth rejoice and be jubilant! Let the people declare among the nations, The Lord reigns! Jehovah is King and He reigns now! Yahweh rules!

Let the sea roar and all of the things in it! Let the oceans, teaming with life, resound with thunderous applause. Let the fields leap for joy. Let all that is in the field, the crops and all of the produce, burst forth with praise. Then shall the trees of the wood sing out joyful songs. Let the trees in the forest rustle with praise before the Lord. Let them exult at Yahweh's approach. They will sing because of His coming. He is on His way to set things right. They will shout in triumph for He comes to judge and govern the earth. They will sing for joy at the Eternal's Presence. He comes to rule the earth. He will judge the world with justice and rule the people in faithfulness.

Oh, give thanks to the Lord for He is good. His grace continues eternally. His mercy endures forever. His message of love never quits. His steadfast love is everlasting. His age abiding loving-kindness is forever. His covenant love does hold true.

 PROVISION

Love of Mine—If I have provided so beautifully for the good earth, know that I have also provided for you in abundance. I have provided for every need but so much more extravagantly than your need, both at home and abroad in the world. You will never lack in any good thing. Your only lack will be in the area of the unwanted, the undesirable and the unnecessary but not in the needed, the desired and the wanted. You can rest in My provision. I AM the Provider and I have provided well for you. It is My joy to meet your need and delight you with an abundant surplus over and beyond the need. This is an area where you can have complete rest. It has been done. I have taken care of it for you.

Because you look to Me as your provider and you trust in My provision, you don't have to spend your life trying to make ends meet or spend your hard earned funds for that which doesn't satisfy. It is a tactic of the enemy, to keep those, who listen to his voice, so busy trying to meet financial demands that, they think, they can't afford to stop and listen to My voice and follow My leading. Those, who follow Me will never lack any good thing. They and their children will never have to beg for bread. They will live in peaceful, comfortable dwellings. They will lie down and rest in perfect peace and rise up and live a full, rich, abundant life.

My Beloved will have plenty to meet the needs of their generous hearts. Their surplus will nurture those less fortunate around them and be an example of My extravagant provision for the abundant life I have promised to My Beloved.

Beloved Bride, would I leave you in pain and suffering? No! Never! Would I allow you to be in anything less than perfect health? Of course not! Would I neglect and not take care of My Own? By no means! My promises are true. They are Yea and Amen! Would I promise a maybe? You can not only put all of My promises in the bank, you can continually spend them. You can claim them as your very own and use them and yet they are always there waiting in the bank for you to use, day and night, with an unlimited amount and supply. So many have an unlimited bank account waiting, ready to be spent with only their signature lacking and yet, they walk around in total poverty seeking the provision and the funds they already have. They only have to open My Word and find the promises and claim them. There are unlimited, breathtaking riches waiting to be used. My Word is truly a treasure house for those willing to seek and find and claim their unlimited, abounding riches. My Word is a gift of My enduring, everlasting love and provision.

2 Corinthians 9:8–11

God is perfectly able to enrich you by making all grace, every favor, all goodness and earthly blessing come to you in abundance so that you may always, under all circumstances, on all occasions and whatever the need, be self-sufficient, possessing enough to require no aid or support. He is able to furnish you, in abundance, for every good work and charitable donation.

God has the power to provide for you richly with an overflowing measure of all good gifts. He will shower all kinds of blessings upon you so that you will always have all that you need for every conceivable need. All of your wants, of every kind, will be supplied at all times. From your overflowing blessings, you will be able to shower all kinds of benefits upon others. You will be able to give of your ample and abundant supply to every work of mercy, every kind act and good cause.

As it is written, Scripture says, The benevolent person scatters abroad. He gives freely and liberally to the poor. His righteous deeds of justice, goodness, kindness and benevolence will stand fast, endure, remain, abide and go on forever. Deeds of charity last forever and will never be forgotten.

And God, Who provides seed for the sower and bread to eat for food, will also provide and multiply the seed you sow and your resources for sowing. He will increase the crop of your charities and the fruit of your righteousness, which manifests itself in active goodness, kindness and charity. He will give you all the seed you need and make it grow so that there will be a great harvest from your goodness. The seeds you sow will bring the yield of a harvest, of the satisfying bread, of good deeds done. You will be enriched in all things, in every way, so that you can be generous on all occasions. Your generosity will bring forth thanksgiving to God. The more you are enriched by God—the more scope there will be for generous giving. You will be rich with plenty left over to share with others, enough for every kind of generosity. People will thank God for what you have done with overflowing, widespread thanksgiving and glory to God. God will give you many opportunities for good and He will produce a great harvest of generosity in you. You will be so enriched that you can give even more generously. When you give your gifts to those who need them, they will break out in joyful thanksgiving to God. You will be wealthy and blessed in every way so that you can be generous in every way, producing great praise and abundant and bountiful thanksgiving to God.

God loves and gives to people, who love to give.

Psalm 37:25

I have been young and now I am old and in all my years, I have never seen the Lord forsake the one, who loves Him. As long as I can remember, good people have never been left helpless. Not once have I seen an abandoned believer. I have never seen the uncompromisingly righteous forsaken or the virtuous deserted, nor have I ever seen the children of the godly go hungry or have to beg for food. Instead, the godly are able to be generous with their gifts. They lend generously and freely to others. They always have something to give away and they give gladly. They always have something to bless their families with. They are ever merciful and compassionate. All day long, they are gracious and show kindness. Their descendants are a blessing and will be blessed.

 PEACE

Beloved Bride of Mine—Be at peace. Don't feel guilty about My precious and special gift to you. Great and abiding peace have those, who love My law and nothing shall offend them. You shall dwell secure in a safe place of peace and blessing. I have chosen this safe place to bless you and surround you with quiet and rest. I promise, I will minister to you as you rest in Me. It will not be an idle time of doing nothing but a very productive time as

I restore, rejuvenate, regenerate, reinvigorate, redeem, repair, refresh and rekindle that which has been injured and torn apart and damaged by the world. I will heal and recreate into My image all over again. You may think nothing is being accomplished in a time of rest but more is being accomplished than you would ever dream. Just receive My love poured out upon you, for I, truly, care about even the smallest detail. I know what you need even before you ask. I AM in the healing, restoring business and I AM at work while you rest and receive.

I will not allow the enemy to come in with a spirit of confusion and anxiety. I will help you to take one step at a time with great faith, in the right direction and with perfect peace. Rest and again I say, Rest. I will guard your peace. I will stand over it and protect it from anyone or anything that would come to steal from your vast, unlimited supply of perfect peace. You will be an example of My gift of peace. I won't let you lose My gift of peace. I will find it again for you. It is yours and no one and no thing can take it from you. Nothing will steal your peace when I AM standing guard over it.

When you lose your peace, stop what you are doing and look up. Check with Me and get back on course. Peace is My way of guiding and directing you in the way you should go. I lead with perfect peace. Blessed are those attuned to My voice. They will never lose their peace when they are following My leading. Peace is My precious, priceless gift to My Beloved.

There is no way to perfect peace, except through Me. Without My abiding Presence and My constant loving care, you could search for a lifetime, taking wrong roads and turns, dead-end streets and back alleys, trying to find peace but the road to perfect peace leads only to Me. I promise, I will see that My special chosen ones, who are listening to My voice and trusting in Me, will have an abundant, constant supply of My perfect, undisturbed, blessed peace.

Isaiah 26:3

You, Lord, give true peace to those, who depend on You because they trust in You. You will guard and keep in perfect and constant peace those, whose mind is stayed on You—those, whose thoughts are fixed on You. A person, whose heart and desire rests in You, You preserve and guard in safety. You, Lord, give perfect peace to those, whose faith is firm.

This is the plan decreed—You will guarantee peace. You will protect and prosper steadfast souls, for they rely on You.

The Lord will stand guard over, sustain and keep, always, in His peace those, whose minds are firmly fastened on Him. Because they commit to Him, lean on Him, hope confidently in Him and trust in Him forever, they will have perfect peace.

Psalm 119:165

Peace is the reward of those, who love Your law and nothing shall offend them. Those, who love Your teaching enjoy well-being. They encounter no adversity or infirmity. There is great and lasting peace for those, who love Your teachings. You give peace of mind to all, who love Your laws and nothing can make them stumble or fall.

Isaiah 32:17–18

The work of righteousness will be peace, internal and external. The effect and result of righteousness will be quietness and calm. The yield of righteousness will be confident trust and blessed assurance, forever.

Integrity will bring peace. Honesty and truth bring us welfare. Justice and right will produce calm, safety, security and bring peace, forever.

My people will live in safety—quietly at home in secure abodes. My people will dwell in peaceable habitations and safe homes, in quiet resting places of comfort. They will abide full of ease in houses of peace, undisturbed in a tranquil country. My people will live in a peaceful place, in secure neighborhoods, in untroubled, calm resting places of hope.

Psalm 85:10–13

Love and truth belong to God's people. Goodness and peace will be theirs. Unfailing love, truth, mercy and lovingkindness have met together. Righteousness and peace have kissed each other—loyalty and peace embrace—justice and peace join hands—victory and peace will unite—grace and truth will come together—steadfast love and faithfulness will join together.

Truth will sprout from the ground and spring forth from the earth. On earth people will be loyal to God. Righteousness looks down from on high, kindness smiles down from above and mercy shines down from Heaven.

The Lord will give His goodness and earth will give its crops. Yes, the Lord will certainly give what is good and our land will yield its increase, producing a harvest of wonderful, bountiful crops. Yes, the Lord will grant us blessing. He will pour down blessings upon us. The Lord, Himself, will give His benefits.

I Will Provide for You

Yahweh grants and gives prosperity.

Righteousness and goodness shall go before the Eternal and shall make His footsteps a path to follow—a way in which to walk. Justice will walk before Him, treading out a path. Salvation will walk along the way of His steps. Victory is marching before God—peace is following in His footsteps. Yes, the Eternal brings us blessing. He will establish His ways upon the earth.

 TASTE AND SEE

Dear One—I thank you, for coming and waiting and listening. Thank you, for being My voice and My heart beat in this last day. So few cherish and treasure time, alone, with Me when I have such love for them and long to share My heart with them. If only they knew what priceless gifts are left unopened because of the pressures of this world and trying to please and follow after the ways of the world. My ways are so far over and above and beyond earthly wisdom. My burden is light and easy.

I only ask that you set time apart and come and commune with Me. Our sweet communion will reap an eternal reward as I share and tell you of My love for you. Come and partake of the cup of My salvation and redemption. Let us break bread together. I invite you to taste and see that the Lord is good and time, alone, together is a priceless treasure worth seeking. What can be more valuable than our communion?

Psalm 34:8–10

O taste and see that the Lord, our God, is good! Open your mouth and taste, open your eyes and see how good God is! Examine and see for yourself the goodness of the Lord. See for yourself, the way His mercies shower down on all who trust in Him. Try the Eternal and you will find Him kind. See how kind He is! Discover for yourself the lovingkindness of the Lord. Blessed, fortunate, to be envied is the one, who trusts and takes refuge in Him.

Blessed are you, who run to Adonai. Happy is the one, who takes shelter in Yahweh. Come to Him for protection and you will be glad. Oh, the joys of those, who trust in Him! If you trust the Lord, you will never miss out on anything good. Those, who turn to the Eternal, will lack no good thing.

Honor the Lord! You are His special people. No one, who honors the Lord, will ever be in need. Let the Lord's people show Him reverence, for those, who revere Him, will have all they ever need. The reverent never want for anything. Revere Yahweh, you His holy ones! O fear the Lord, you His saints, His consecrated ones. Revere and worship Him for there is no want to those, who revere and worship Him with godly fear. Worship God if you want the best. Worship opens doors to all His goodness.

Rich men have become poor and hungry and the great may suffer poverty and want in need but those, who seek and search for the Lord, shall not want any thing.

Even strong, young lions sometimes lack food and suffer hunger but those, who inquire of and require the Lord, by right of their need and on the authority of His Word, none of them shall lack in any beneficial thing. Young lions on the prowl get hungry but God seekers are full—of God.

Unbelievers, apostates and renegades may be famished and starving but those, who turn to the Lord, are never in need. They have everything they need. They want for no good thing. They have every good thing.

Psalm 119:103

How sweet are Your words to my taste, sweeter than honey in my mouth! How pleasing are Your promises and Your teachings to me!

1 Peter 2:2–3

Like newborn babes, you should crave, thirst for and earnestly desire the simple, pure teachings, the unadulterated spiritual milk of the Word of God. By the Word of the Lord, you will be nurtured and grow up, mature and whole, thriving upon it to your soul's health. Surely, you have already tasted the goodness and the kindness of the Lord!

Psalm 33:4–5

The Word of the Lord is right and all His works are done in truth and faithfulness. His every deed is faithful! Everything He does is worthy of our trust. The promises of Jehovah are reliable and dependable. The Word of the Lord holds true and all His works endure. The Word of Yahweh is correct and straightforward and all He does springs from His constancy and goodness. He loves what is right and fair. He cherishes virtue and honesty. He loves whatever is just and good.

The earth is full of the goodness of the Lord. The earth is full of the Lord's faithful care. His mercy and grace fill all the earth. The earth is full of the lovingkindness of the Lord. Yahweh's unfailing, steadfast love fills all the earth.

Psalm 31:19

Oh, how great is Your goodness, Lord! You have treasured up Your goodness for all, who fear You. How wonderful are the quantities of good things You keep for those, who revere You! What great blessings You have in store for those, who honor You! What a wealth of kindness You bestow on Your worshipers! How vast is Your goodness! How abundant is the good that You bestow!

You have done so much for those, who come to You for protection, blessing them before the watching world. Your great goodness for those, who take refuge in You is right before people's eyes, in sight of all. Adam's descendants watch as You reserve Your kindness for those, who love You. You have made manifest Your goodness for all, who turn to You for shelter. Everyone knows how good You are and how securely You protect those, who trust in You.

What blessings are ready and waiting for all, who run to You to escape an unkind world!

Psalm 86:5

You, O Lord, are good! You are ready to forgive our trespasses, sending them away, letting them go completely and forever. You are plenteous in mercy and grace and abundant in loving-kindness to all, who call upon You. You have great, abounding and steadfast love for all, who invoke You and ask for Your aid. Your constant love is always there for those, who pray to You. You are rich in faithful love. Your unfailing love never fails. Lord, You are so good to us!

 COUNTED

My Own—Yes, I care more for you than you will ever know. I have even the hairs of your head numbered. If I

*have such a small thing as a hair counted and numbered,
know and rest assured that I care about your life and I
have a wonderful plan to bless you, in even the smallest
detail. Truly, I have scattered your path with flowers and
delights and surprises and gifts of My love. I will continually surprise you with My love. I will rain down blessings
on you, too numerous for you to count or comprehend.*

*Bask in My love. Soak up the rain of blessings. Enjoy
and savor My gift of life and life abundant. I say of My
creation of you, It is good. It is very good. You don't have
to continually strive to obtain or maintain My love. I
promise, it will never leave you or be diminished or be
less in any way. Simply rejoice that you are counted
among the Beloved. You are cherished and chosen and I
AM well-pleased with you.*

Luke 12:6–7

Are not five sparrows sold for a penny, next to nothing? Yet,
not one is uncared for, or neglected in God's watch-care. Not
one has escaped God's notice. He has everyone of them in mind.
Not one has been forgotten. Not a single sparrow will fall to the
ground without your Father's knowledge—without His consent
and permission or outside your Father's care. God has never
overlooked a single one.

As for you, the very hairs of your head are all numbered. All
have been counted by God. He takes every single hair into His
reckoning. Fear not! Be not seized with alarm or struck by fear.
There is no need to be afraid. Don't be afraid of anything. Cease
being anxious or intimidated, you are far more precious than

many flocks of sparrows. You are of far greater worth and surpass the importance of many sparrows. He pays much greater attention to you—even down to the last detail.

Psalm 139:17–18

How precious it is, Lord, to realize that You are thinking about me constantly! I can't even count how many times a day Your thoughts turn toward me. When I awake in the morning, You are still thinking about me.

How precious are Your thoughts to me, O God! How I prize Your thoughts! How deep and rare and beautiful, I find Your thoughts, O God! How vast the sum of them! If I could count them, they would be more in number than the sand. I can no more count them than I could count the sand of the sea. How immeasurable are Your concepts, My God! How inexhaustible their themes! How precious have Your desires become to me, O God!

Psalm 90:12

Teach us to number our days so that we may apply our hearts to wisdom that we may gain the heart of wisdom. Teach us to count our days rightly and take it to heart that we may obtain a wise heart. Teach us to count up the days that are ours, to count every passing day and to order our days rightly. Help us to make the most of our time and to use wisely all the time we have. Help us to acquire a discerning mind that we may know how to interpret our existence. May we grow in wisdom and become wise. Teach us how short our life really is and help us to live wisely and well.

Psalm 40:5

Many, O Lord my God, are Your wonderful works! How numerous, O Lord, Your wondrous deeds! Many are the wonders, which You have done for us. I will tell others about the miracles You have wrought and Your wonderful care of us. How many are the plans You have for us! You have planned so many marvelous things for us. Your wonderful purposes are all for our good. Richly have you worked out Your wondrous purposes for us. Who can count Your thoughts toward us? Many are Your us-ward thoughts!

Great things You have done! If I should declare and speak of them, they are more than can be counted, too many to number. If I tried to recite all Your wonderful deeds, I would never come to the end of them. There is too much to tell! I could never speak of them all. Their number is too great—beyond number. Were I to recount them, they would pass all count. I want to speak of them again and again but they are more than can be told.

Neither numbers nor words account for You! Eternal One, my God, there is no one like You!

Psalm 9:1–2

I will praise You, O Lord, with my whole heart. I will recite and count Your miracles, one by one. I will recount all of Your marvelous works. I will tell aloud Your wonderful deeds.

I am happy and jubilant because of You. I will give thanks and sing a hymn of praise to Your name, O Most High. I delight in You!

 CARE

Dear One—My tender loving care is a manifestation of all of the love that is in My heart. It is something you can experience. You can see, touch and feel it. My great love cares for your safety and protection in every situation. It covers all areas of provision. It reaches to your health and well-being and all areas of your life, right down to the smallest detail. It includes a peace that passes all understanding, at all times. It

seems so difficult for My loved ones, My very Own, to realize that they can, truly, relax and really trust and have faith in Me. So few sit back and enter into My blessed Sabbath Rest and savor and enjoy life to the fullest. The worst offense, to the perfect peace I have promised, is those who try to figure things out with their minds and prepare for the worst. Don't they realize all of the love in My heart for them and that they should prepare for the best because of all of My promises to keep them close to My heart and care for them? Very few look up and thank Me ahead of time for the best that is on the way.

You are one of the few. You thank Me for what is and for what is on the way. You are grateful ahead of time for what is coming. You trust in My love and in My perpetual loving care for you. You anticipate with joy that the very best is yet to come. Your faith in Me will bring great rewards and very special surprises and gifts of My love. It shows Me how much you care for Me.

Yes, Love of Mine, I will continually rain down blessings on you for I delight in delighting you. Blessed be the day of My visitation and this is that day! There will be no more days without My loving Presence and My loving care surrounding you. Truly, you will lack in no good thing. I will supply your need, even before you ask, for I care about you. Bask in My love. Delight in My continual rain of blessings. You are cherished and chosen and very well cared for. I love you.

Hebrews 2:6

What am I that you are mindful of me—that You visit me and You graciously and helpfully care for and look after me? What am I, a mere mortal—that you concern Yourself with me and watch over me with such loving care?

Isaiah 46:3–4

I was the Maker and I will be the Bearer. I made you and I will bear you. I have created and cared for you since you were conceived. I have supported you since you were born. You have been carried by Me from the womb. I will be your God through all your lifetime. Yes, even in your old age, I will be the same. When your hair is gray, I will ever uphold you. I made you and I will care for you. I will sustain you and deliver you. I will rescue you and bring you to safety. I will be responsible for what I have made. Yes, I will always take care of you and keep you safe. I will be your Savior. I AM the One, Who has done this and I will continue. I shall carry you and save you. I will take care of you.

1 Peter 5:7

Turn all your anxiety over to God. Unload all your burden on Him since He is concerned about you. Cast every worry you have upon Him. Deposit with Him, once and for all, the whole of your worry. Cast the whole of your care, all your anxieties, all your worries, all your concerns on Him, for He cares for you affectionately and cares about you watchfully.

He makes you His care. You are His personal concern. He is always concerned about you. His great interest is in you. He cares about what happens to you and He is most careful with you.

Cast all your cares upon Him, for He cares for you.

Luke 12:24

Be carefree in the care of God. Look at the birds of the air. They are free and unfettered. They are not tied down to work. God takes care of them. You count far more than the birds. You are much more valuable to God than birds. Don't be uneasy, anxious or worried about your life. It is the Lord's pleasure to give you the Kingdom.

Luke 12:31

You must make God and God's goodness your greatest care. More than anything else, put God first and do what He wants you to do—then all other things will be yours as well. Steep yourself in God and You will find that all of your everyday cares will be met by Him. Don't be anxious about tomorrow. God will take care of all of your tomorrows.

HIS EYE IS ON THE SPARROW

Chorus:

I sing because I'm happy. I sing because I'm free.
For His eye is on the sparrow and I know He watches me.
His eye is on the sparrow and I know He cares for me.

Why should I feel discouraged? Why should the shadows
  come?
Why should my heart be lonely and long for Heaven and
  home?
When Jesus is my portion, my constant Friend is He.
His eye is on the sparrow and I know He cares for me.
Chorus

Whenever I am tempted—whenever clouds arise,
When songs give place to sighing, when hope within me
  dies,

I draw the closer to Him—from care He sets me free.
His eye is on the sparrow and I know He cares for me.
Chorus

Let not your heart be troubled—His tender word I hear
And resting on His goodness, I lose my doubt and fear.
Though by the path He leads me but one step I may see.
His eye is on the sparrow and I know He cares for me.
Chorus[1]

---

[1] Civilla Martin, *His Eye Is On the Sparrow*. Public domain.

Chapter 3

ℐ Will Protect You

 FEAR NO EVIL

My Own—I will keep you safe and secure under My wings. I will guard you and watch over you. I will surround you with My loving care. I will keep you safe from all harm and any attack or plan of the enemy. No weapon that is formed against you will prosper. The slings and arrows of your enemy will have no effect. You can rest secure in My protection and My provision. I will keep you safe from all evil. I will deliver you from even the fear of evil. It will not come near you. In a day of darkness, even gross darkness, you will be free to go where I send you with joy and rejoicing and great and undisturbed peace. Your trust and faith and freedom, to move out in all of My promises to you, will bless a multitude. So, go with an impenetrable shield of My loving care surrounding you. The enemy will not stop you, or even slow you down, with thoughts of fear. He will not imprison you by causing you to seek a place of safety. The center of My will is the very safest place you can be. Your courage and trust and faith will grow as you step out in faith—taking one step at a time. You will find

that, truly, every promise is a sure possession. It has been tested, tried and proven.

You are protected, surrounded, enclosed and enveloped within My watchful, loving care for you. Rest in My love.

Isaiah 41:10–13

I AM your God. Fear not! There is nothing to fear—for I AM with you. Don't be intimidated or alarmed. Do not be dismayed. Don't look around you in terror. Stop being anxious and watchful—for I will support you. I will strengthen and harden you to difficulties. I will embolden you. I hold you with My saving right hand. I will uphold you and retain you with My vindicating, victorious right hand of rightness and justice. I will hold you with a firm grip. Yes, I have helped you and I will help you. I will make you strong and give you victory.

Behold! All, who hate you, will be disgraced. Those, who attack you, will vanish into thin air. Those, who rage against you, shall be put to shame and confusion. Those, who strive against you, shall be ashamed and confounded. Those, who fight against you, will be destroyed and perish. Those, who are incensed and inflamed against you, shall be as nothing. All, who defy you and vent their anger against you, will come to naught and offer no resistance. Those, who pick quarrels with you, will be humiliated. All, who set themselves against you, will be disappointed.

You shall seek those, who contend with you but shall not find them. You will look for your assailants but they will not be there. Those, who war against you, shall be as nothing, nothing at all. You will look for them in vain, for they will all be gone. When you go looking for your adversaries, you won't find them—not a trace of your enemies, not even a memory.

For I AM the Lord, your God, I hold and firmly grasp your right hand. I AM not letting go! I AM the Lord, Who says to you, Fear not! I have become your Helper. I whisper to you, Do not be afraid. I will support you and save you.

1 John 4:18

There is no fear in love—dread does not exist. Full-grown, complete, perfect love turns fear out of doors. There is no room for fear in love.

Fear brings with it the thought of punishment. The one, who is afraid has not reached the full maturity of love's complete perfection and has not yet reached the full measure of love.

Isaiah 54:17

No weapon that has been forged or fashioned or made to harm you will succeed. No instrument made to attack you will prosper or prevail against you.

Every tongue that accuses you in judgment will be refuted. You shall prove false every accusation against you. You shall rout every charge brought against you and show it to be wrong. Words spoken against you won't hurt at all. No word spoken against you shall win its plea. You will have an answer for anyone, who accuses you. This is the lot and the fortune of the Eternal's servants.

The eternal promises are the triumph I will award them. They shall triumph through Me, declares the Lord. In the eternal promises, do I maintain their cause. Their vindication is from My hand—it comes from Me, affirms Jehovah. This is the very word of the Lord. It is Yahweh, Who speaks. I, the Lord, promise to bless you with victory.

Psalm 23:4

Even though I walk through a valley of deepest darkness, a ravine as dark as death, a deep, sunless valley of the shadow of death—I will fear no evil. My road may run through a glen of gloom but I will not dread or be afraid of danger, disaster or harm for You are close beside me.

I am reassured by Your rod that protects me and Your staff that guides me. They comfort me and give me courage. Your strength and support are, indeed, my comfort and courage. I'm not afraid when You walk at my side. You make me feel safe and secure.

Psalm 3:3

You, O Lord, are a shield that surrounds me. You are my glory and the lifter of my head. You are my Protector, my Defender, my Champion, my Strength, my Sustainer, my Help and my Hope.

You raise my head and hold it high. You give me great victory and honor. You are my wonderful God, Who gives me courage.

1 Thessalonians 5:15

Make sure that no one ever pays back one wrong with another. Instead, always try to do what is good for each other and for everyone. Don't be hateful to hateful people—do good. Never repay evil for evil, aim at what is best for everyone.

Romans 12:21

Do not let yourselves be mastered, conquered or overcome by evil but master, conquer and overcome evil with good.

2 Thessalonians 3:2–3

May you be delivered from the unjust, the perverse, unprincipled, improper, unrighteous, the unreasonable and the wicked—for faith has not reached all hearts. May you be preserved from actively malicious, unbalanced people, the wrong headed and wrong hearted—for not everyone loves the Lord, not everyone has faith and is held by it and not everyone is worthy of trust but the Lord is, truly, worthy of trust. Yet, the Lord is faithful. He keeps faith with us and can be relied on. He will strengthen you and establish you. He will set you on a firm foundation and guard you and keep you from every attack, of every kind, from the evil one. He will protect you and fortify you from all evil. The Master never lets us down. He will stick by you and protect you from all harm.

Psalm 91

1. I dwell in the secret place of the Most High. I abide under the shadow of the Almighty. I rest and repose in the shelter of the Lord. I live as a ward of the God of Heaven and earth. I will stay and remain fixed and stable under the protection and defense of God All-Powerful, Whose power no foe can withstand.

2. I will say of the Lord, You are my sheltering haven, my refuge and my fortress—my place of safety. You are my God, in You will I trust.

3. The Lord will keep me safe from all secret traps. Certainly it is He, Who rescues me from the hunter's trap, the snare of the fowler and every treacherous lure. He will keep me safe from every wasting disease, every deadly epidemic and every destructive pestilence.

4. He will spread His wings over me and cover me with His feathers. Under His wings, I take refuge. I find shelter within His protecting power. His huge, outstretched arms will protect me. Under them, I am

perfectly safe. His arms fend off all harm. His truth will encompass me with armor. His constancy and fidelity are my assurance of security. His faithful promises are my encircling shield and my protection.

5. I will not dread or be afraid of the terror of the night or of any danger that is abroad in daylight. I will not fear nocturnal terror or the evil that kills in daylight.

6. I will not fear the conspiracy that spreads in darkness or the plague that stalks in the dark. I do not fear the epidemic or sickness that devastates at midday. I am not afraid of the calamity or sudden disaster that spreads havoc at noontime.

7. A thousand may fall at my side and ten thousand at my right hand but it will not come near me. I, myself, will remain unscathed. The plague will never reach me. I will not be harmed.

8. I will witness the sinner's reward. Only a spectator will I be, myself inaccessible in the secret place of the Most High. I will stand untouched and watch it all from a distance. Only with my eyes will I behold the recompense of the lawless. I will only look on and see how evil men are punished. I will gaze upon and take careful notice of the reward of the wicked.

9. I have made the Lord my defender. He is my refuge, my shelter, my fortress and my protector. The Most High is my habitation and my dwelling place. I run to Him for safety.

10. No terrible disaster will strike me or my home. No

violence will happen near my home. No scourge or plague will even come near my dwelling. No evil will befall me. No disaster or calamity will overwhelm me. No misfortune will be sent to me.

11. He will give His angels orders regarding me. He will command His angels to guard and protect me wherever I go and keep me in all my ways.

12. By their power, they will uphold me, lest I should even injure my foot on a stone. They will carry me in their arms and bear me up in their hands.

13. I can walk over reptiles, the most deadly snakes and I can overpower the strongest lions. I will kick lions and snakes from my path.

14. Because I, truly, know You and I have set my love upon You, You will deliver me. Because I cleave to You and anchor my love in You, You will rescue me and all those who cling to You. You will lift me beyond danger. I will have Your protection. Because I know You by Your name, You will keep me safe.

15. When I call to You, You will answer me. You will be with me in trouble and deliver me and honor me. In hardship and affliction, You will be at my side and bring me safety and deliverance.

16. You will give me life, long and full and let me see Your saving care. You will even let me participate in Your salvation and see Your saving power.

2 Timothy 1:7

God did not give us a spirit of cringing, fawning fear that makes cowards of us. The Spirit, God has bestowed on us is not a spirit of cowardice that shrinks from danger. No, it is a Spirit, which results in our being filled with His power and divine, self-sacrificial love and a calm, well-balanced mind. He has given us sound, good judgment, discipline and self-control.

God's gift, the Holy Spirit, does not want you to be shy or timid with His gifts or to be afraid of people but to love people and enjoy being with them. He wants us to be bold and strong, loving and wise and to inspire strength and love and wisdom in others.

Psalm 121:7–8

The Lord will protect you from all evil. He will preserve your life and your soul, now and forever. The Lord keeps watch over you as you come and go. He will guard your going out and your coming in. He will watch over you when you leave and when you return. God guards your very life! Yahweh will keep you from all harm. The Lord will protect you and keep you safe and secure from all dangers, now and forever—henceforth forevermore!

 TROUBLE

Peace, My Dear One, peace. Let not your heart be troubled. Don't let your heart race ahead and worry about what might happen. Sufficient for the day is the trouble thereof. Don't borrow tomorrow's trouble that might not even come. I can, truly, say and mean with conviction, don't worry—be happy! As you rest in Me and have faith and trust in Me, you will realize and rejoice that I AM totally dependable.

You will learn to walk on the water of tomorrow. You will walk into the unknown and into a future that looks unsure, as if it were a solid firm foundation—the terra firma of the soul. Don't worry or fret or be anxious about what might come. Don't prepare for a future calamity that will never come to you. Don't spend your time and money preparing for a day that never comes—when I have promised you plenty and abundance, over and beyond your need. I have promised a future of good, with all things working, together, for your good.

I have covenanted with you My eternal, unconditional love and My tender, loving care and guidance through any storm of life. Rest and be at peace, trust in Me and in My love. I love you.

Matthew 6:34

Take no thought for the morrow. Sufficient for the day is the trouble thereof. Take the trouble of each day as it comes. One day's trouble is enough for one day. There is no need to add to the troubles each new day brings. Don't be anxious about what tomorrow might bring. Make up your mind to stop worrying. Don't begin to worry. Enough of worrying! God will help you deal with whatever hard things come when the time comes.

Psalm 50:15

Call upon Me in a day of trouble and I will deliver you and I will be glorified. I want you to trust Me in your times of distress. Call to Me for help in your hour of need and I will come to your rescue. I will strengthen you and you will thank Me and praise Me and give

Me honor. Pray to Me when trouble comes and I will save you.

Psalm 37:39–40

Yahweh protects His people. The upright have the Lord for their Savior. He is the One, Who saves. The salvation of the consistently righteous is of the Lord. He is their Refuge and secure Stronghold in the times of trouble. Help comes from the Eternal. Deliverance comes from Him. The Lord helps and delivers them from the wicked because they trust in Him and have sought refuge in Him. He will stand by them and rescue them and save them.

When we run to Him, He saves us. God-strengthened, we are delivered from evil.

Psalm 34:17–19

The Eternal turns His eyes toward the righteous. His ears are open to their cry. When they cry, the Eternal listens and He rescues them from all their trouble.

The Lord's people may suffer a lot but He will always bring them safely through. The Lord hears His people when they call to Him. When they cry out for help, He delivers them out of all their distresses and troubles. People, who do what is right, may have many problems but the Lord will solve them all.

Though hardships without number may beset the upright, Yahweh rescues them from them all.

Psalm 46:1–4

God is on our side! Jehovah is our Protector, our Shelter, our Refuge and our Strength. God is our mighty Fortress. He is always ready to help in times of trouble, when we need Him. He is a very present and well-proven help in trouble or distress.

Yahweh is a soon found help, an always ready and reliable help, to be found without fail when trouble occurs. He is, most surely, found in any distress.

Therefore, we fear not though the earth be shaken and the mountains plunge into the depths of the sea. For this cause we will not fear, even when the earth quakes. Though the earth be transformed or even removed, we will not be afraid. Though the seas seethe with raging waves, though they roar and foam and heave in turbulence, we will not fear. Even if the world blows up, we need not fear. God All-Powerful is with us and fights for us. Yahweh, Saboath, the Lord of Hosts, the Commander of the Heavenly Hosts is here among us. The God of Jacob, our Defender, has come to rescue us.

Psalm 107:19–20

They cry to the Lord in their trouble and He saves them from all of their troubles. In their adversity, they cry out to Yahweh and He delivers them from their distress, from their evil plight and peril. He snatches them from the door of death and destruction. He sends forth His Word and heals them. He gives the command and they are cured. He gives an order to preserve their life. He saves them from dying and the grave. He speaks and rescues them from all dangers.

You were in trouble but you prayed to the Lord. In your desperate condition, you called out to God and by the power of His Own Word, He healed you and saved you.

Isaiah 43:1–2

The Eternal, the Lord your Maker and your Life-Giver, the One, Who created you and formed and fashioned you says, Fear not! Don't be afraid. I have saved you. I have taken up your cause and brought you to Myself. I have redeemed you. I have ransomed you instead of leaving you captive. I have called you by your name. You are Mine. I have made you Mine—My very Own.

When you pass through deep waters of great troubles, I will be with you. When you pass through the sea and through rivers of difficulties, they will not overwhelm you. They will not sweep you away or swallow you up. You will not drown, for I will be with you. When you walk through the fire of oppression, you will not be burned or scorched. The flames will not consume you. They will not kindle upon you or harm you. You will not suffer, for I AM Yahweh, the Lord, your God, the Holy One of Israel, I AM the Eternal, the Majestic One, I AM Jehovah your Deliverer, I AM your Savior and I will be with you.

Nahum 1:7

The Lord is good! He is our strength, a stronghold and a hiding place. In a day of trouble He knows and understands everyone, who trust in Him. The Lord protects His people. Yahweh is better than a fortress. He is a haven for all, who seek refuge in Him. He cares for all, who seek shelter in Him. The Lord is good to all those, who hope in Him. He welcomes everyone looking for help— no matter how desperate the trouble.

2 Corinthians 1:3–4

Blessed be God, the Father of our Lord Jesus Christ, the Father of all mercies and the God of all consolation, Who shows compassion at all times. Let us give thanks to God from Whom all help comes. He is the Source of every comfort and encouragement. He, Who is ever-giving comfort, comforts us whenever we suffer in our afflictions and every time we have trouble. He enables us to comfort others with the same comfort and consolation that we have received from Him. The Father of sympathy and pity encourages us to encourage and help those, who are in any kind of trouble or distress. Praise be to God, Who helps and supports us in every hardship, so that we can be there for someone else when hard times come—just as God was there for us.

STARS

Beloved Bride—I will hold your hand and lead you in a way like no other. I will give you eyes that can see in the dark but I will also hold your hand and lead you through the darkness. The coming darkness will cause you no fear. My perfect love, for you, will cast out all fear. For you, this present darkness will be an opportunity to help bring in the Last Great Harvest. I AM the Lord of the Harvest and I will usher in a mighty and uncountable harvest. Don't take the time to try to count them. They will be coming from all directions and places, in vast numbers.

Those sitting in darkness will get up and run to the light. Those caught up and engulfed in darkness will clamor for the light and the light of My coming.

My Stars, My Chosen Ones, will shine bright in the darkness and point the way to Me. They will be beacons and lighthouses in the dark, stormy seas. They will rejoice that they were chosen for such a time as this. For My Chosen Ones, this will be a time of great joy in the Great Harvest.

You have been prepared for this great day. You are fit and ready, now, for service. I promise, you were chosen for such a time as this. Don't fear or dread the coming darkness but welcome it as a necessary part of the Last Great Harvest.

Look up and rejoice! Your Redeemer draws near and His love will light your way and His loving care will keep you safe.

Behold! I AM coming soon to catch My Bride away! And you will be ready. You will have plenty of oil for your lamp and you will respond with joy, Behold! My Bridegroom comes!

Philippians 2:15–16

Show yourselves to be blameless and guileless, innocent and pure, uncontaminated and irreproachable Children of God, without blemish—faultless, in the midst of a crooked and wicked generation, among a people that are perverted and perverse. Shine, like the stars in the universe, lighting up the night sky—while living in a dark and evil-disposed, depraved, deceitful, warped and twisted, diseased world.

You are seen as bright stars, heavenly lights, luminaries shining out clearly in a dark world. Let your light shine brightly before them. Shine out like beacons of light, holding out to them the Light of Life.

Hold fast to the Message of Life that proclaims where Life is to be found, for you are holding in your hands the very Word of Life. Shining like stars, hold out to the dark world and offer them, the teaching that gives Life, for you are to them the Light of Life.

Go out into the world, uncorrupted, a breath of fresh air in this squalid and polluted society. Provide people with a glimpse of good living and of the living God. Carry the Light and the Life-Giving Message out into the night.

Isaiah 42:5–7

This is what the Lord says—the only true God, Adonai, the Eternal, Yahweh, Who created the heavens and stretched them out, Who spreads out the earth with all that it produces and brings forth and bears, Who gives vital air and breath, life and spirit to everyone in all the world, the Source of all life is the One, Who says—In My grace, I have summoned you. I, the Lord, have called you for a righteous purpose, in righteousness. I have called you for the victory of justice. I have selected you and sent you to bring My promise of hope. I have created and formed you for rescuing My people. I will take you by the hand and keep you. I will firmly grasp your hand and support you. I will strengthen you and protect you as you go. I will appoint you as My promise to the people. I will give you, for a covenant, to the people. I send you as My light to the nations, to give sight to blinded eyes. You will be a light to shine for all the people.

You will bring forth the bound ones from the house of restraint and free the captives from their bondage. I, Yahweh, have called you to serve the cause of right. I will guard you as you free the prisoners, from dungeons of despair and darkness.

Luke 1:78–79

Because of the faithful love of our God and through the heart of tender mercy and the lovingkindness of our Lord, a Light from Heaven will dawn upon us. In the deep, heartfelt compassion of our God, the Sunshine from on high will visit us. God's Sunrise will break upon us. The Light of Dawn will beam on us from Heaven and shine on and give light to those who live in darkness, under the cloud of death. The Lord will cause the bright Dawn of Salvation to rise on those of us, who live in the dark. A new day will dawn on us from above. This Light from Heaven will guide us into a life of peace. It will show us the way, directing our feet, one step at a time. Heaven's Dawn, the Dayspring from on high, will visit us and shine upon us. God's love and kindness will shine upon us like the sun that rises in the sky.

Matthew 4:16

The people, who live in a country of shadow, as dark as death, have now seen a great Light. The people, who have spent their days shrouded in darkness, upon them has the Light shined. On those living in the region where death constantly casts its shadow, the Light has broken through upon them.

On those sitting and dwelling in darkness, in the midst of the shadows of death, a brilliant Light will dawn and arise upon them.

Daniel 12:3

Those, who are wise counselors, the teachers and leaders, who have guided people to the true path, will shine like stars in the brightness of the firmament forever. The people of God, who turn many to righteousness and right standing with God, will give forth light and glitter and shine brightly like the splendor of Heaven's dome. Everyone, who has led others to please God, will stand out and glow like stars for all eternity.

Matthew 5:16

Be light-bearers! Let your light so shine before others that they may see your moral excellence, your praiseworthy, noble and good deeds and the beauty of your life. Then they will recognize the Source and they will give honor and praise and glory to your

Father, Who is in Heaven. Let your good works glow and shed light for all to see. Be a light for others. Live so that they will see and give praise and glory to your Heavenly Father.

Isaiah 60:1–2

Stand up and shine! Rise up in splendor! Rise clothed in light! Yahweh beams upon you. The Lord shines on you. Arise from the depression and prostration in which circumstances have kept you. Rise to a new life! Shine! Be radiant, with the glory of the Lord, for your light has come and the glory of the Lord has risen upon you!

For behold, darkness shall cover the earth and dense, gross darkness and deep gloom shall cover all the people but the Lord shall arise upon you. His glory and His splendor shall be seen on you. His sunrise glory breaks upon you. Though thick dark clouds shroud the nations, your new day is dawning. People will see His glory around you. Arise and be glad! The Eternal shines brightly upon you!

TRUTH

My Own—I will take your hand and gently lead you into all truth and the truth will set you free from fear. It will set you free from fear of the unknown. When you have My wisdom to rely on, you see with eyes of faith into the unknown. The truth will set you free from the fear of failure. When I AM leading, I will never lead you to fail but I will lead you to be victorious in every situation. You can depend on My leading you to succeed. It will set you free from the fear of man. When I AM on your side who can rise up against you? Who dares to come against My Beloved, when I AM their Protector and Defender? My love and my loving care are a protective shield round about them.

You will not listen to the voice of the enemy or fall into the deceits and the deceptions of his lies when you are walking in the truth. You will be free, indeed! There is great peace and security in truth. It will save you from the entanglements, snares and the traps of the enemy.

Recognize, know and embrace the truth of My Word. It is a gift of My love for you.

Psalm 19:7–11

7. The Torah of Adonai is perfect. The law of the Lord is complete. It is an undefiled law, restoring the whole person, refreshing and reviving the spirit, renewing life, promoting spiritual vigor and converting the soul. The revelation of God is whole and pulls our lives together. The signposts of God are clear and point out the right road. The teachings and rules of the Lord can be trusted. They give new life. The Lord's instruction never fails. His teachings endure and last forever. The testimonies and decrees of Jehovah are sure and faithful, trustworthy, reliable and confirmed. They give wisdom to ordinary people. They make the ignorant, the simple and the foolish—wise.

8. The teachings of the Lord are true, making people happy. The statutes of Jehovah are right, rejoicing the heart. The precepts of Yahweh are just, a joy to the heart. The instructions of the Lord are correct—they

make our heart glad. The Eternal's orders are pure—they make our heart rejoice. The life-maps of God are right, showing the way to joy.

The commandment of the Lord is radiant and enlightening, giving insight to the mind. His commandments shine clear and bright, they light up the way. His directions are plain and easy to comprehend. The instruction of the Lord is lucid, making the eyes light up.

9. Reverence and respect for the Lord is good. It will last forever. The reverent fear of the Lord is clean and pure, enduring forevermore. Worshiping the Lord is sacred. He will always be worshiped.

10. The judgments of the Lord are true and righteous altogether. The Eternal's rulings are upright and altogether just. The decisions of Yahweh are correct and faithful. His ordinances and rules are completely fair. More to be desired are they than gold! Yea, than much fine gold! They are more precious than many precious stones and more to be prized than the finest and purest gold. His words are sweeter also than the honey that drips from the honeycomb.

11. By Your teachings, Lord, I am warned—by obeying them, I am greatly rewarded. By them, Your servant is enlightened, taught, reminded, instructed and illuminated. Your servant pays heed to them and is careful to do them and very diligent in keeping them—thus, is Your servant formed by them.

John 8:31–32

If My Word abides in you, if you are faithful to what I have said and hold fast to My teachings, if you live in My Word, if you dwell in the revelation I have brought—you, really and truly, are My disciples and you will know the truth and the truth will make you free.

If you make My Word your home, if you abide in My Word and live in accordance with My Word, you will understand and experience for yourselves the truth and the truth will free you.

John 17:17

Sanctify them—purify, consecrate, separate them for Yourself and set them apart for holiness. Make them pure and holy by teaching them Your words of truth. Your Word is truth—the message is true. Make them ready for Your service. They will be truth-consecrated in their mission. Your Word is holy, consecrating truth!

Luke 1:37

With God nothing is ever impossible! No word from God shall be without power or impossible of fulfillment. There is not a thing God cannot do! Every promise from God shall surely come true. God's promises can never fail. No promise of God can fail to be fulfilled. God can do anything!

WORD

Love of Mine—Bask in My love in this day of discovery— this blessed day of finding hidden treasure in My Word. I will reveal My love for you, as you hunt for treasure in My Word. It will be a special time of joy, as you discover and find and rejoice anew over what has been there all the time. There is a vast field of treasure all around you, at all times.

So many walk on past and don't stop and dig for treasure in My Word. It is gems and jewels and nuggets of gold. It is riches beyond imagining! Thank you, for stopping and digging and exclaiming with delight and joy over each treasure. I appreciate your search and I will see that it does not go unrewarded. I will lead you and guide you, as you seek and search the Scriptures. I will bless a multitude with what you have discovered in this day of discovery, this time of revelation, this treasured time of finding that you are treasured and very precious to your Beloved.

As I sustain you with fresh new manna daily, you will come to know that no one lives, truly lives, by bread alone but by every Word that proceeds from the mouth of God. You will be so thrilled with what you discover in My Word! You think, you know and understand My Word now but you haven't even scratched the surface. You will be so surprised to find that this priceless gem and that true treasure was there all the time. Just as My love is without measure, the depth of My Word has never been fathomed. It is always fresh and new and yet ageless, ancient and eternal. From everlasting to everlasting are the promises, the unsearchable wisdom and the priceless treasures that you will find in My Word. It, truly, is the earthly connection with Heaven that you can hold in your hand. It is alive and active and sharper than any two-edged sword. It is fresh daily bread from Heaven that will feed you and sustain you and nourish you. It will grow you up to maturity and give you life abundant. It is health and healing and the way to wholeness and holiness. My Word will show you the way. It will lead you and guide you along the road of life—the pathway to Heaven.

My Word, truly, is a love letter to you and to all who will open and read, to those who will listen and hear the Word from Heaven. Those, who long to draw closer to Me, have only to open My Book and they will find Me. I will always be right there with them—explaining and amplifying and sharing and testifying about My Word. My very Presence will be right there with them—loving them and drawing them closer still, encouraging them and helping them. Anyone who will open My Book will always find a very present help in time of trouble. They will find a simple and easy to read road map that will show the way. It will answer all of your questions with the wisdom of the ages.

My Word will bless your life. It is an eternal, heavenly declaration of My unconditional and everlasting love for you.

Deuteronomy 8:3

Food is not people's only need. It takes more than bread to stay alive. It takes a steady stream of the Words from God's mouth. Men and women can live on what proceeds from God's mouth—His decrees, His commands and His every declaration.

The Lord put you through hard times. He brought afflictions on you and suffered you to hunger so that you would feel your need of Him. He disciplined you and humbled you with hunger and then He fed you manna, a food previously unknown to you or your ancestors. He did this to teach you that you must not depend on food alone to sustain you. You need every Word that God speaks. He wants you to understand that real life comes from feeding on God's Word.

Psalm 119:161–162

My heart stands in awe of Your Word. Because of Your Word, my heart thrills, trembles and vibrates with joy. With all my heart, I respect Your Word.

I rejoice in Your laws, like one who finds great treasure. Joyful am I, over Your Word! I am overjoyed at Your promises, like someone who discovers vast treasure. I'm ecstatic over what You say, like someone who strikes it rich. Your promises bring me happiness. I'm as happy over them, as if I had found priceless treasure. I find joy in Your Word!

1 Peter 1:24

All flesh, all earthly life, is like grass and all of its splendor and glory, its honor and beauty is like the flower of grass.

The grass withers and the flower dries up and drops off but the Word of the Lord, the declaration of God, the divine instruction and teaching of the Lord, the Gospel, the Good News remains, endures and lives and abides forever.

Yes, our natural lives will fade as the grass does. All our greatness is like the flower of grass, which falls to the ground but the Word of the Lord, God's Great News, will last forever!

Hebrews 4:12

The Word, that God speaks, is full of power—making it full of life and active, operative, energizing and effective. It is sharper than any two-edged sword, sharper than the sharpest knife. It cuts all the way into us, where the soul and the spirit are joined, to the thoughts and feelings in our hearts, penetrating to the dividing line of the breath of life and the immortal spirit, to the very marrow of the deepest parts of our nature. It exposes us for what we really are. It sifts and analyzes and judges the very thoughts and purposes of the heart. It is a discerner of the secret motives and emotions and intentions of the heart.

Isaiah 55:10–11

Just as the rain and the snow come down from the heavens and do not return without watering the earth, soaking it and making it fertile and fruitful, making it give growth and yield, making it sprout and bud and bring forth fruit that it might give seed for the sower and grain and bread for the hungry—it is the same with My Word. It shall not return to Me void, without producing effect or useless. It will not return to Me empty, without carrying out My will. It will do My will, achieving the end, carrying out the purpose and succeeding in what it was sent to do. My Word never comes back to Me without result but it will perform and accomplish that which I please and it will prosper in the thing for which I send it. My Words don't return to Me without doing everything I send them to do. They will never return to Me unfulfilled or before having carried out My good pleasure and having completed the mission they were sent to do. The Words I speak will make the things happen that I want to happen. My promises will never be fruitless or in vain. My Words will accomplish what I want and achieve whatever I send them to do.

Psalm 119:105

Your Word is a lamp for my feet and a light for my path. Your Word is a flashlight to light the path ahead of me and keep me from stumbling. By Your Word, I can see where I'm going. It throws a beam of light on my dark path!

Isaiah 61:11

For as surely as the soil of the earth brings forth its seed and bursts into spring wildflowers and as a garden cascades with blossoms, so the Lord God brings righteousness into full bloom. The Lord will bring about justice in every nation on earth like flowers blooming in a garden. Before all the world, will the Lord God Eternal bring forth triumph and renown. His goodness and glory will be like a garden in early spring that makes the seed that is sown in it, sprout and spring up and bloom. He puts praise on display before the nations. His praise in the nations of the world will be like a garden filled with young plants springing up everywhere. Everyone will praise Him!

The Lord will cause His goodness, glory and renown, justice, righteousness, victory, triumph and praise to spring up before the nations—through the self-fulfilling power of His holy Word.

Matthew 13:52

See how every student, well-trained in God's Kingdom, can put his hands on anything you need, old and new, exactly when you need it. Every scribe, every teacher of the Law, every interpreter of the Scriptures, the Sacred Writings, the Word of God, who becomes a disciple of the Kingdom of Heaven is like a householder, who knows how to bring forth, out of his storehouse, treasure that is new and treasure that is old. Every student, well-trained in the Realm of Heaven is like the owner of a store, who can put his hands on anything you need, exactly when you need it—quality new things and also things mellowed with age, by reason of use, the fresh as well as the familiar.

2 Thessalonians 3:1

Pray for us that the Word of the Lord may have free course and hold its onward course. Pray that it may speed on, spread rapidly and continue to spread unhindered. Pray that the Word may be glorified, extolled and triumph wherever it goes. Pray that the Word of God will win converts and bring Him glory, proving its glorious power. Pray that the Word will be respected and received with honor.

Pray that the Master's Word will simply take off and race through the country to a groundswell of response!

Matthew 24:14

The Word of the Lord, the Message of the Kingdom, will be proclaimed in all of the inhabited earth. The Gospel, these Glad Tidings, will be preached throughout the whole wide world as evidence and as a witness to all people. The Good News will be announced to the nations so that all nations may hear and be confronted with the truth. When the Word of the Lord has spread throughout the whole earth—only then, the end will, finally, come.

 EVERLASTING

My Own—I will stop your heart from racing ahead to finish. It is true that the end of a thing is better than the beginning but I have also planned for you to enjoy and rejoice in every step of this faith walk that you have stepped out on, taking one step at a time. Each new step will be exciting and different from the last step. Don't run past the special gifts and surprises and delights I have planned along the way. I AM coming soon but I promise there is plenty of time to complete the task at hand and the mission and ministry I have planned for you. A lifetime is plenty of time. Take your time—slow down—relax

and rest in Me. The work is Mine, in fact, I have already done the finished work. It is finished and already written down and recorded, so sit back and watch as the completed work unfolds before your wondering eyes! No striving or straining on your part will finish the work one day sooner or add one tittle or a single jot to the completed work. Simply be a receiver, an anointed vessel, through which I can pour out My love on My beloved Bride so that I can touch their hearts and prepare them for My soon coming. The work is not yours but Mine and it is a finished work—a labor of love.

Dear One, don't force us to do a word, a page, a completed portion of the book every day. That is a wearisome task. Let it unfold in My timing and it will be a joy for both of us. You have entered into striving and straining and you are exhausting yourself. I say, You are doing well and have done well but there will be days of complete rest and times away from the task at hand. There will be plenty of time for you to take care of the other details of your life and keep a balance. I promise, it will be finished on time—in My timing and not a day sooner, not a single minute sooner. No amount of pushing and pulling and striving and straining will bring it about one second before My appointed time—so rest and rejoice.

Be at peace in the deep well of My peace. Draw peace from My well of living water. Continually drink in peace, absorb it, let it become part of you. Enjoy the gifts I AM raining down on you. I AM blessing you with an abundance of peace and rest.

If you will let Me, I will help you keep your office and files and desk clean and orderly and I will help you to keep caught up on domestic chores. They will even become a joy for you, not something you put off to the very last. I promise, you will whistle while you work, sing praises to Me and dance for pure joy! Only after all loose ends and unfinished tasks are done, will we move forward on the book. When your home and your mind are uncluttered, you will again be ready to receive and be a clear channel for Me to flow through.

Stop setting goals for yourself. That is the world's way but it is not Mine. I flow and ebb with a smooth and peaceful calm. Wait! And again I say, Wait on Me. You miss so much when you try to rush ahead. Some of My sweetest gifts are peace and quiet and rest. You aren't trying to meet the goals of a publisher or printer. No one has set deadlines for you to try to reach. The goals are of your own design and plan. Many are the plans in your heart but it is My purpose that prevails and I have planned your purpose with so much love. Trust My timing, as you trust in Me. Have faith in Me.

I know how overjoyed you are at being chosen for this special assignment but I promise, I will not fire you because you aren't working hard enough or fast enough. It is already completed in Heaven. It is finished and you have done well. There is no way I would possibly change My mind or give the job to someone else.

My Own, I will not let you stray, too far, off course. I have promised to be your constant guide and to guide you into all truth and the truth will set you free from all pain and suffering—for I have, already, borne it for you. I have brought you back on course—for your own good and for your peace and joy. I have promised that this will be a time of great peace and abounding joy and I will see that this time is an especially beautiful memory as I send you forth with a special delivery letter—A LONG LOVE LETTER to My beloved Bride.

Stop and absorb all the love being poured out upon you and know that it is an unconditional love. You did not and you cannot earn it by good works and mighty deeds and exploits. It was there from the beginning and it will be there until the very end. From everlasting to everlasting is My love, for those who love Me.

Psalm 103:17

The Lord's merciful goodness and His lovingkindness are from everlasting to everlasting for those, who reverently fear Him and keep His commandments. His faithfulness and His salvation reach to their children's children.

The Lord's love never fails those, who revere and respect Him. To those, who keep His covenants, His love and His goodness continues forever and ever, even to their descendants. Yahweh's faithful love is ever and always, eternally present to those, who worship Him. He makes everything right for those, who follow His guiding principles.

The love and mercy of Adonai are from eternity past to eternity future for those, who earnestly remember His laws—hearing, receiving, loving and obeying them. The steadfast love of the Lord remains forever on those, who hold fast to His precepts and live mindful of them. On those, who follow His covenant ways, imprinting them on their hearts and remembering to do whatever He says, rests the everlasting love of the Lord.

Proverbs 3:11

Do not despise the discipline of the Lord. Do not shrink from or spurn the chastening of Yahweh. Don't resent His correction. Do not become weary or impatient about His rebuke. Do not loathe or abhor His reproof. For whom the Lord loves, He corrects and trains, even as a father corrects the son in whom he delights, his well-loved son, who is very dear to him.

Revelation 3:19

Those, whom I dearly and tenderly love, I tell their faults and convict and convince and reprove and chasten. I discipline and instruct them. So, be enthusiastic, in earnest, burning with zeal and repent, changing your mind and attitude.

All those I love, I rebuke and correct. So, shake off complacency and take correction seriously. Be in earnest and repent. Be eager to do right and change your hearts and lives.

Psalm 139:23–24

Search me thoroughly, O God and know my heart! Look deep into my heart and find out everything I am thinking. Don't let me follow any evil way but lead me in the way that time has proven true—the way everlasting.

Examine me, test me and try me, watch lest I follow any path that grieves You. Point out anything in me that offends You. Probe me and know my mind, my thoughts and my concerns, see if I am taking a wrong course, see if there are any false paths my heart is set on. Make sure there are no hurtful, crooked or wicked ways in me and lead me on the right road to everlasting life.

Psalm 31:14–15

I have trusted in and relied upon You, O Lord. You are My God! My times are in Your hands. My future is in Your hands. My destiny is under Your control. I am trusting in You. I have complete confidence in You, Lord.

Habakkuk 2:3

The vision is yet for an appointed time. These things I plan won't happen right away. Slowly, steadily, surely, the time approaches when the vision will be fulfilled. Though it tarries, wait earnestly for it. If it seems slow, do not despair for these things will surely come to pass. Just be patient. They will not be overdue one single day. The vision hastens toward the end. It will not be late.

Deuteronomy 33:27

The Eternal God is our refuge, our shelter and our dwelling place and underneath are the everlasting arms. The Everlasting God is our hiding place, our place of safety. He carries us in His arms. His arms are beneath us, supporting us. His everlasting arms will hold us forever.

SABBATH REST

Beloved—Truly, My burden is easy and My yoke is light, for you are yoked with Me in a labor of love. You are burdened with an already completed task. This work has already been accomplished in My perfect plan for your life. You can, truly, enter in to My blessed Sabbath Rest when you know that it is a finished work. In My great love for you, I have taken the task and finished the work. My burden amounts to rest and rejoicing in great peace and abounding joy. I have ransomed you from work and redeemed you from striving and straining, for I AM a Savior, Who saves. I save not only to eternal life but I save from anything that would rob you of the peace and joy I have planned for your life. Treasure the rest—My rest—My beautiful, blessed, holy Sabbath Rest.

I will be with you and I will hold your hand and gently lead you through this productive, peaceful time. The burden is not yours. I have already taken it from you. Rest in My promise of peace. Rest in restoration of body, mind and soul. This work will be more like play than work. You will enter into it with anticipation of joy and gladness and great and abiding peace. It will get better and better as you go and grow. Truly, the end of a thing is better than the beginning and the very best is yet to come. Be not concerned but rest, in amazement, as My plan unfolds before your wondering eyes. I invite you to enter into My blessed Sabbath Rest in this labor of love.

Thank you, for being a willing vessel and a clear channel through which I can pour out My love to My Body—My beautiful Bride. I will always give you only one message to share and that is—tell them that I love them.

Blessed One, I do not condemn your weakness. I commend it, for You always turn to the right Source for help and strength. You will receive an ample and abundant supply. You can trust Me and depend on Me and lean on Me. I AM faithful to all of My promises and so much more. I reach far beyond all of My recorded promises to bless you. I AM there at your time of need, with all that you will ever need—all of the help you will need in any situation. Be at peace. I will turn everything to your good and My glory. You can rejoice and thank Me for whatever happens. It will always be a time for good and growth. I have a plan to bless you and minister peace and wholeness and great and abiding joy to you. You will be comforted in My plan for restoration and healing. Be of good cheer! I can right any wrong—better than before. You will see that there are, truly, no mistakes in My Kingdom but I am working all things for your good, internally, externally and spiritually. They will come together in a perfect whole. You will be able to look back and see that what looked like terrible mistakes were a part of the perfect plan for your life. You will see how I can turn what the enemy of your soul meant for evil into great good. I will heal every wound inflicted by the enemy and there will not even be a scar remaining—no reminder of past hurts. Don't continually fight the enemy. Simply look to Me and rest in Me. I AM your Savior, I AM your Redeemer and I AM your Defender. Being in a continual battle would not be the perfect peace, at all times, that I have promised you. Rest and rejoice as I turn everything to good in My perfect plan for your life.

Rest and watch and see how I delight in delighting you. See how I have taken care of all of your needs. I have given life to your life and peace to your rest. Rest in peace and be not anxious about anything, for I know your needs even before you ask. I AM in the process of moving Heaven and earth to meet every need, in abundance. I have covenanted with you health and wholeness in body, mind and soul. I will take care of all of the details, as you rest in Me.

Entering into My Sabbath Rest, means not ever leaving it again. It is not a state that you enter and leave and return to but once begun, it is an unending blessing and a continual state of being. Sit back and rest as you watch My perfect plan unfold before your wondering eyes. Gaze in wonderment and rejoice forevermore! I AM in control and I won't let anyone or anything interfere with My perfect plan for your life. I invite you to enter into My blessed Sabbath Rest—a gift of My everlasting, unconditional love for you.

Hebrews 4:9–10

There is still awaiting a full and complete Sabbath Rest reserved for the true people of God—a promised Sabbath of rest for God's people. The one, who has once entered God's rest has ceased from the weariness and pain of human labor just as God rested from those labors peculiarly His Own. To enter this place of rest is to rest from your own works. God, Himself, is at rest and we will surely rest with God.

Exodus 33:14

The Lord said, My Presence will go with you and I will give you rest. I, Myself, will go along with you and give you victory. I will bring you to your resting place of peace. I will lighten your burden. I will put you at ease. I will settle you safe. I will give you success. I will go in the lead and I will lead you. Set your mind at rest.

Isaiah 30:15

The Lord God, the Holy One of Israel says, In returning to Me and resting in Me, you shall be saved. Your salvation lies in tranquility and your strength in serenity. Your victory shall come about through calm and confidence—your triumph by stillness and quiet trusting. You can be strong by being quiet and resting in Me. Be calm. Hope and trust in Me and you will be strong.

Matthew 11:28–30

Come unto Me, all you, who labor and are heavy-laden and over-burdened and I will cause you to rest. Come to Me, all, who are tired and weary from carrying heavy loads—all, who find life burdensome—all, whose work is hard and whose workload is heavy, I will lead you into rest. I will ease and relieve your souls. I will refresh you.

Take My yoke upon you and learn of Me, from Me. Let Me be your Teacher. Accept My teachings. The teachings that I ask you to accept are easy. I AM meek and lowly, gentle and humble of heart and you will find relief and ease, recreation and blessed quiet and rest for your souls. My yoke fits perfectly. The yoke I give is kind and pleasant. It is comfortable and gracious. My yoke is wholesome, useful and good—not harsh, hard, sharp or pressing. My burden, the load I ask you to carry, is light. The burden that I ask you to bear is easy to be borne.

Isaiah 11:10

His dwelling shall be glory—His rest glorious!

Psalm 116:7–9

Return to your rest, O my soul, for the Lord has dealt bountifully with you. Now I can relax and be at rest, once again, for the Lord has done wonderful miracles for me. Return, O my soul, to your tranquility, regain your composure, for the Lord has been good to you. I don't need to worry anymore. My heart is at peace, once again.

The Lord has delivered my life from death, my eyes from tears and my feet from stumbling and falling. He has rescued and liberated me. He has saved my life from peril and banished my tears and weeping.

I will walk before the Lord in the land of the living. I will conduct myself in a godly manner in the midst of human society. I shall live. Yes, in His Presence here on earth.

I will rest and trust in You, Lord.

Chapter 4

I Will Give You a New Life

FAITHFUL

Faithful Love—You see! With spiritual eyes, the plan I have for you looks beautiful—a plan to be anticipated and embraced. That is what walking by faith is all about. This spiritual view of your life will guarantee constant permanent peace and joy abounding, abiding and overflowing. Your trusting faith walk allows My plan to flow freely. A walk of doubt and dread and fear, hinders and holds back My perfect plan. Thank you, for embracing My plan for your life. Thank you, for anticipating, with joy, all that I have in mind for you and for saying and meaning with all of your heart, Here I am Lord, send me and use me! Thank you, for being a channel of blessing that I can freely use, day and night, to pour forth blessing to My beautiful, cherished, beloved Bride.

Love of Mine, you have been faithful over a little and now I set you over much. I have found you trustworthy and dependable and faithful in your love for Me. Your being faithful is a gift of your love to Me. Because of your faith in Me, you gladly step out in faith and joyfully follow My leading. Your faith and trust will grow as you find Me totally trustworthy and faithful. It is a very necessary and needed part of love—to have confidence in one another. Thank you, for your confidence, My faith full, faithful Bride.

Thank you, for being faithful and full of faith. Thank you, for stepping out into the unknown, believing and trusting and having great faith. I will greatly reward you for your great faith and faithfulness—to Me, to My Word, to the task at hand and to all that I set before you. You step out joyfully, believing. You thank Me ahead of time for what you see with eyes of faith. It is conclusive evidence that it is on the way. Your looking with eyes of faith, allows Me freedom to answer your prayer even before you ask. Your faith in My perfect plan for your life, your trust in My tender, loving care for you and your belief that even though it is not seen, it is on the way—is the perfect way to pray. Pray in faith, believing.

Your faith is an expression of your deep and abiding love for Me. It is received with love and returned with great love for you, My faith full, Faithful One.

I want you to trust in My love and to have faith in My love. I promise, it will always be there. It is a sure possession. You can depend on My love. You can lean on it and stand on it. It is a firm foundation that will never be shaken or removed. My love is not anything like human love that can be removed and shaken and is often untrustworthy, deceitful, self-imposing, self-gratifying and self-centered. The earthly version of love, so often, is clouded and dim and obscure but My love is pure and sure and trustworthy. I have proclaimed My love for you in the heavens and on earth. My Son came to share and tell you of My love. He came to show you how to love and to show you the intensity of My sacrificial love. My Holy Spirit continually woos and draws and tells you of My love.

I will reveal to you the beauty of My love in holiness, for My love is a holy and a beautiful experience. Trust in Me. Have faith in My love. Forget all of the pain and suffering, the sorrow, the wounds and scars of human love and look to Me for I AM trustworthy. I will, always, faithfully love you.

Psalm 37:23–24

When your life pleases the Lord, He gives you a sure footing. When your steps follow the Lord, God is pleased with all your ways. He sets your course. Your steps are ordered, directed and established by the Lord. By the Lord, are steps made firm. Progress comes from the Lord. He will make sure every step you take is sure. The Lord, Himself, will watch over your every step. When your ways delight the Lord, the Lord delights in every detail of your life.

Though you fall, you will not lie prostrate. You are not down for long. The hand of the Lord will lift you up. Though you stumble, you will not be utterly cast down, for the Lord grasps your hand in support and upholds you. The Lord is a support, to which you can cling. The hand of the Lord will sustain you. The Eternal is holding your hand. God has a grip on your hand.

Hebrews 11:1

Now faith is the blessed assurance, the confirmation, the title deed of the things we hope for, being the proof of the things we do not see and the conviction of their reality. Faith perceives as real fact what is not revealed to the senses. Faith is the confidence of knowing that what we hope for is real and does actually exist and the conviction, of the reality, of things that as yet are out of sight.

Hebrews 11:6

Without faith, it is impossible to please God because anyone who comes near to Him must believe that He exists and that He rewards those who diligently seek Him. You must have faith that He will reveal Himself to all, who draw near to Him.

Hebrews 10:22–23

Let us all come forward and draw near to God by faith—by that leaning of the entire human personality on God in absolute trust and confidence in His power, wisdom and goodness. We can now, without hesitation, walk right up to God in the Holy Place. Jesus has cleared the way by the blood of His sacrifice. Let us come, full of faith, remembering that He is, always, faithful to His Word.

2 Corinthians 5:7

We walk by faith. We walk not by sight or appearance. Faith guides our steps, not sight. We guide our lives by faith, not by what we see. We live by believing not by seeing.

Deuteronomy 7:9

Know, recognize and understand that the Lord, your God, is God indeed! He is the Faithful God, Who keeps His covenants. He is true to His agreement of steadfast, loyal love and lovingkindness. He is merciful and gracious to those who love Him and keep His commands. You can depend on Him. He is trustworthy. So, love Him and obey His commandments. He will faithfully keep His promises to you and your descendants for a thousand generations.

1 Corinthians 1:9

Faithful is God! He is entirely trustworthy. You can rely on Him. He can be depended on. He is ever true to His promise.

He is the One, Who invited you into wonderful friendship, fellowship and companionship, to share the life of His Son, Christ Jesus, our Lord. You were divinely summoned into a joint participation, to be partners with and share everything with our Lord Jesus Christ.

Matthew 25:21

The Lord says, Well done! Good job! You did well. You have been faithful. You are trustworthy. You have shown yourself to be worthy of trust and you have proven that you can be trusted. You are good, excellent, loyal, honorable, admirable and upright. Since you have been faithful with a small amount, in small things and ways, I will make you ruler over a large amount. I will entrust many things to your care and responsibility.

Enter now into the joy of your Lord! Come and share the delight, the blessedness and the happiness with Me. Let us celebrate the feast together!

Psalm 149:4–5

The Lord loves His people. He will beautify the meek and humble with salvation. The Eternal takes pleasure and delights in His people. Adonai is pleased with those that are His. He adorns the lowly and afflicted with salvation garlands. He crowns, the wretched and oppressed, plain folk with victory. Yahweh is kind to His people conferring victory on those, who are weak. He will beautify humbled ones.

Let the Lord's Beloved rejoice in the glory and beauty, which God confers upon them. Let the faithful rejoice, gloriously, in this honor. Let the saints be joyful. Let the godly triumph in glory. Let the true lovers of God break out in praise. Let them sing aloud from wherever they are sitting. Let them shout for joy even in bed.

All of you faithful people exult in glory as you worship Him, praising God to the heights with your voices. Celebrate and worship!

GOOD WORK

My Very Own—Thank you, for taking this special time and coming into your prayer closet and closing the door. This is a time of Holy Communion as I share My heart with you. Long ago I chose you to be the vessel to receive this love letter to My Bride. Just as delivering and sending My holy Word has been pure joy, this long love letter will be an added dimension and will bring an even greater portion of joy and gladness. This time of preparation will not be a sacrifice but a time of anticipation and expectancy, of hope and faith, as you trust in Me to complete the good work I have started.

Be at peace in this special, set apart, time of rest and restoration. I AM coming soon but there is plenty of time to finish and distribute a very special love letter to My Bride. Don't get in a hurry. Take time to treasure each day as it comes. Take one step at a time, one day at a time. Take time to enjoy the moment.

Even as all stages of the butterfly are equally important for the beautiful transformation, each stage of this development is necessary and important for the meta-morphosis of a new assignment. Behold! I make all things new—in My time. I AM preparing and transforming My Bride for My soon coming. My Bride will be ready with plenty of oil for their lamps for the joyful cry, Behold! The Bridegroom comes!

Surely, I will give you a double portion of My love, poured out on you to overflowing. As you carry and deliver My love letter, My love will spill over and splash over on all who come near. It will require no effort on your part as I impart My message of love to My beautiful, beloved Bride. My love will melt the hardest heart and open closed and locked doors. It will be an armor and an armory of weapons of light against the deepest darkness and rage and hate. I will disarm hate with love and over-come evil with good.

You will rejoice as My love flows out through you to others. It is My love they seek so desperately, following the wrong paths. When they experience My unfathom-able love, they will turn from darkness to light. They will follow after the light, knowing that My love is what they were looking for all along. So rejoice in the labor I have chosen for you—a labor of love.

Philippians 1:6

I am confident and fully convinced with settled and firm per-suasion—I am quite sure of this very thing that He, Who began a good work in you, will continue performing and perfecting it and carry it through, to a successful completion, until the day of Jesus Christ—right up to the time of His return. He will keep right on developing that great good work, helping you to grow in grace until His task within you is finished. God, Himself, is the One, Who began so noble a work in you and I am certain He won't stop before it is complete.

2 Corinthians 5:19

God was in Christ offering peace and forgiveness to the people of the world and He has given us the work of sharing His message about the peace we can have with Him. His work for us is to tell, proclaim and preach the wonderful news. God reconciled the world to Himself and He has given us the message of reconciliation. He invites us to enter into His work of making things right. He will not hold us guilty for our sins. He will not charge our offenses, misdeeds and transgressions to our account. He has entrusted us and ordained us to speak the Good News.

1 Timothy 6:17–19

Don't set your hopes on the uncertainty of wealth, or the riches of the world's goods and money, which are untrustworthy. Set your hopes on God, Who richly and ceaselessly supplies and provides us with everything for our enjoyment. He richly endows us with all of the joys of life. The Lord generously gives to us all that we need for our happiness. He furnishes us, in full measure, with all things so that we might be rich in noble deeds and good works.

Do good. Be rich in good works. Show kindness. Find your wealth in lovely deeds. Be open-handed and generous-hearted. Practice benevolence. Be liberal and ready to share with others what God has given to you. Exhibit a wealth of good actions. Sympathize with those in distress—be willing to communicate and ready for fellowship with them. Be ready to distribute freely.

Use your money to do good.

In this way, you will be laying up for yourselves riches that endure forever. You will make for yourself a good, solid foundation for the future. You will build a treasure that will last—amassing for yourself treasures in Heaven and gaining life that is, truly, life—life indeed, life that will last forever, everlasting life.

Titus 2:14

The Lord sacrificed Himself on our behalf that He might redeem us from all unrighteousness, lawlessness and iniquity and purify, for Himself, a people to be peculiarly His own—a people, who are eager and enthusiastic about living a life that is good and filled with beneficial deeds for others. He offered Himself and gave His life to free us from a dark and rebellious life and give us a good, pure life, cleansed from all sin. He makes us His very Own people, His Own treasure, a people He can be proud of, who are ambitious and energetic in goodness, zealous of good works and noble deeds and whose hearts are pure.

John 9:4

We must work the work of the One, Who sends us and be busy with His business while there is daylight. Night is coming when no work may be done. The task laid upon us is that so long as day lasts, we should perform deeds that have their source in Him, Who has sent us. All of us must quickly carry out the task assigned to us because there is little time left before the night falls and all work comes to an end. Let us work while the sun shines, work will be over when night falls. While daylight lasts, we must be busy with the work of the Sender.

2 Timothy 3:16–17

Every Scripture is God-breathed and given by His divine inspiration. Its aim is to make us fit for any task. Through God's Word, we are put together and shaped for the tasks God has for us. Every Scripture passage is useful for instruction, for reproof, for conviction of sin, for correction of error and resetting the direction of one's life. It is for showing what is wrong with our lives, for correcting faults, for teaching right-living and for training in holiness that results in living in conformity to God's will—living a life that has God's approval in thought, purpose and action.

The Scriptures are God's way of preparing us in every way so that we will be competent, well-qualified and fully equipped for any and every kind of good work.

1 Corinthians 3:9

We work together with God and you are God's work. We are fellow workmen, partners, joint promoters, and laborers together with and for God. We share God's work as co-workers.

You are God's garden and vineyard, His field to be planted. You are God's farm under cultivation. You are God's building being built, a structure of God's design. You are God's good work.

Philippians 2:13

God is the One, Who is constantly putting forth His energy in you. It is God, Himself, Whose power creates within you both the desire and the power to execute His gracious will. God is all the while effectually at work in you energizing and inspiring your will into action. He makes you willing and gives you the energy to do what He wants, to do His good pleasure and His delight. God in His goodwill enables you to fulfill and achieve His good purpose in pursuit of His gracious design. God is always at work in your hearts producing in you the desire, the intention and the power to work His good work. God gives you the desire to obey Him and helps and enables you to obey Him.

Be reverent and sensitive before God. Be energetic in your life of salvation. That energy is God's energy deep within you. God, Himself, is willing and working what will give Him the most pleasure. God works in you both will and deed, making you willing and able.

RECREATION

Beloved—I, carefully, created you in your Mother's womb. I loved you even before you were conceived. Even before the foundation of the earth, I had you in mind. When you caught your very first breath of life, I was there breathing life into you, not only physical life but spiritual and eternal life. At that very moment I was there, carefully, watching over you and caring for your every need and sending others to love you and care for you and watch out for you. Not just your parents and grandparents and relatives but there were so many others that I sent to minister to your needs and carefully care for you. I was so pleased with you at your birth that I said of My creation of you, It is good. It is very good!

Blessed be the day of your birth and rebirth! I will, continually, breathe new life into you and recreate you anew daily. Do you realize that new birth is continually going on in your body? Of the trillions of cells I have created, each one is being renewed, restored and totally made new and fresh continually. The body is being renewed, the mind is made new and the soul and the spirit are refreshed and strengthened daily. Even while you are at complete rest, new life is being rebirthed, healing is taking place, refreshing and restoration are all going on. I not only created you, I continually recreate you into My likeness and image.

I have used the events of your life to shape and form you and prepare you for these days. You are well prepared for such a time as this. You will be grateful for even the difficult days and hard times of your life, knowing they were days of preparation. Without having passed through the storms of life, you would not be ready for such a time as this. So rejoice in the good times and the bad and see your life as a perfect whole, all coming together in wholeness and holiness. Rejoice with Me in the continual creation of you. Embrace your uniqueness. You are not one of many but you are the only one and I have made you well. I rejoiced at your birth and I rejoice in the continual rebirth that is all the while going on.

Yes, My beautiful Creation, I will continually surprise you and delight you with my love. You have a special gift and a unique talent for enjoying the beauty of My creation. I will lead you to share with others, who will learn to savor My blessings that are continually raining down on them but they walk right past them and don't even notice. From you, they will learn to slow down and take time to smell the roses and enjoy the fragrance and the uniqueness of each one.

Relish and totally enjoy each breath of spring and the wonder of new life emerging in a myriad of ways. Rejoice in the beauty of the fresh new green of spring—the lovely flowers, the beautiful butterflies and all of the surprises and delights of My creation, budding and blooming and

*breaking forth in resurrection power. I have created but
I also continually recreate and renew and rejuvenate. Be
exceedingly and continually glad in this time of recreation
and let Me recreate you into My image and likeness.*

Ephesians 2:10

We are, truly, God's Own handiwork, His workmanship. He
made us. We are His design. We are God's making—God's work
of art. We are God's masterpiece—recreated, created anew, born
anew in Christ Jesus. He has recreated us through our union with
Christ and invited us to join Him in the good work that He does.

We have been created for a life of goodness, taking paths,
which God prepared ahead of time for us. His plan is for good
works to be the employment of our lives. He plans for us to live
a good life—doing the good things He has always wanted us to
do—living, as He has always wanted us to live.

Psalm 139:13–16

You, alone, created my whole being. You formed me in my mother's womb. I will praise You for the awesome wonder of my birth.
Like an open book, You watched me grow from conception to birth.
All the stages of my life were spread out before You. All the days of
my life were foreseen by You and set down within Your book, before
they ever took shape, before I had even lived one of them.

Truly, You formed my inward parts and my innermost being.
My substance was not hidden from You. Your eyes saw my
unformed substance when I was made in secret. You knew me
through and through—my being held no secret from You. You
saw my bones being formed. My frame, being shaped in a secret

place, was not hidden from you. I was being intricately and skill-fully woven as if embroidered with various colors in a region of darkness and mystery.

I give thanks to You that I am fearfully and wondrously made. I praise You that I am awesomely, amazingly, miraculously cre-ated. I worship in adoration. What a creation! Wonderful are Your works! For so many marvels, I thank You. A wonder I am and all Your works are wonders!

2 Corinthians 5:17

When someone becomes a Christian, they are a brand new person. They are not the same anymore. A new life has begun. Anyone united with Messiah gets a fresh start, created anew. Anyone in union with Christ is in a whole new world—the past has passed away, everything has become fresh and new. When you are engrafted in Christ, you are an altogether new creation. The old previous moral condition, the old way of living has disappeared. A new way of living has come into existence— a resurrection life that is far better than you have ever known before. A new life has come into being!

Psalm 119:40

Behold, I long for Your precepts and teachings. In Your righ-teousness, give me renewed life. In Your justice, give me life anew. Revive me through Your saving goodness. Quicken me with new life in Your Word. Your commands and guiding principles give me new life.

1 Peter 1:23

Your new birth comes from God's living Word. You have been regenerated, born again, not from a mortal origin but from One that is immortal, by the ever living and lasting Word of God. You have been born again through God's everlasting Word that can't be destroyed—new birth by His Message that lives forever. The Good News is what the Lord has said—what He has said will stand forever.

Just think of it! A life conceived by God, Himself! Born again by the incorruptible Word of God, which lives and abides forever—the Message of the living, everlasting God, which endures and lasts forever.

Genesis 1:32

And God saw everything that He had made and behold it was very good. His creation was fitting, suitable, pleasant and admirable and God approved it completely. God looked over all that He had made and He saw that it was excellent in every way. It was good. It was very good. Indeed, it was very good!

Revelation 21:5–6

He, Who is seated on the throne said, See! I make all things new. I AM making the whole of creation new. He also said, Record this. What I AM saying is accurate, trustworthy and incorruptible. And He further said, It is finished. It has been accomplished. I AM the First and the Last, the Beginning and the End, the Alpha and the Omega, from A to Z. I AM the originating cause and the One, Who brings things to their consummation and conclusion.

To anyone, who is thirsty, I will freely give the Water of Life from the Well of Life.

FEARFULLY AND WONDERFULLY MADE!

You are a marvelous, awesome creation of God— fearfully and wonderfully made!

The body has over one hundred trillion cells—each knowing its own function and being constantly renewed and recreated.

The circulation system comprises sixty thousand miles of tubing. There are so many capillaries in the body that laid end to end, they would ring the equator more than twice. If the nerves were laid end on end they would extend for more than two thousand miles.

The absorptive surface of the intestine is about thirty square miles.

The average person has twenty feet of skin, which wears away and is replaced every few weeks. One square inch section of skin contains: twelve feet of blood vessels, eight hundred pain sensors, four hundred sweat glands, twelve thousand nerve endings, forty-eight heat sensors and one hundred pressure sensors.

Fifteen million red blood cells are being produced every minute and sent on various missions such as carrying oxygen and nutrients for body building and removing wastes and toxins.

The human eye and brain are too awesome to record here! Read about them and thank God for creating you so amazingly and wonderfully well!

 RESURRECTION

Beloved—I promise I will resurrect you on this Resurrection Day. As you trust your life to Me I will resurrect you into wholeness and divine health. You are right! I never intended for My Bride to walk hand in hand with infirmity. I never planned for my Bride to become more and more susceptible to the enemy's plundering and robbing and stealing

the very life from My Beloved. I intended for life to become sweeter and sweeter in every way as you walk hand in hand with Me and entrust more and more to My loving care. As you draw closer and closer to Me, you will come to rely on the fact that I AM, truly, Jehovah Rophe, God your Healer, Who heals. At the same time I AM a Savior, Who saves from every affliction. I even took all of your infirmities and sicknesses on My Own back when I suffered affliction, in the wounds I bore for you.

You need not have any dread of growing old, infirm, weak and dependent when I promise you supernatural strength, divine health, wholeness and wisdom beyond your years. I promise, the very best is yet to come. Life will become better and better, not worse and worse. It will become more precious and abundant in every way, every day. Because you have chosen Me and put your faith and your trust in Me and because of your love for Me, you can depend on the fact that I will not turn you over to the devourer but I will rebuke the devourer for your sake. Don't let the enemy fill you with dread of what he might possibly do to you, when I have promised life and life abundant in every way and every area. I have promised a life free from worry and anxiety and fear. I promise a peace that passes all understanding—a peace, the world can't even understand. I promise to keep you in My loving care, free from all harm. Anticipate with joy, all of the good gifts I have prepared for you—even resurrection life daily.

Proverbs 3:1–2

Do not forget what I teach you. Always remember what I tell you. Ever keep in mind My law. Guard My principles and lock them in your heart. Let your heart keep My commandments. Keep My instructions, My directions and My rules in your memory, store them in your heart and obey them completely, for abundant welfare, plenty and prosperity will they give you. Peace and tranquility, inward and outward, will they bring you. A long, happy life continuing through old age till death, will they add unto you. They will help you to live a satisfying and successful life—lived full and well and long.

Jeremiah 30:17

I will restore health to you and heal your wounds, the Eternal promises. I will bring back your health and you will get well. I will put a bandage on you and cure your wounds. I will heal your injuries. I will heal every scar of yours. I will cause new skin to grow, declares Yahweh. For you, I will come with healing, curing the incurable.

Psalm 92:12–14

Good people will prosper and do well. They will stay healthy and grow strong.

The uncompromisingly righteous shall flourish like the palm tree. They will be long-lived, stately, upright, useful and fruitful. They will bloom like the date palm.

They will grow to the greatness of the cedar in Lebanon—majestic, stable, durable and incorruptible. They will be planted in the house of the Lord Jehovah. Transplanted into the Lord's Own house, they will take root and flourish in the courts of our God. They will blossom in God's courtyards. Growing in grace, they shall still bring forth fruit, even in a ripe old age. Vigorous and sturdy shall they be! They shall be full of spiritual vitality and rich in the virtues of trust, love and contentment. They will remain fresh and green to proclaim Yahweh's integrity. They are living memorials to show that the Lord is upright, mighty and faithful to all of His promises. Such witnesses to our God!

They will say about You, Lord, The Lord is just and He always does what is right. He is my Protector in Whom no fault can be found. He is my mighty Rock in Whom there is no wrong. He is my Strength, Who never errs. There is nothing but goodness in Him!

Jeremiah 17:7–8

Most blessed are you, who believe in the Lord and rest your confidence upon Him. Blessed are you, who hope in the Lord and trust in Him. The Lord will show you that He can be trusted.

You will be like a tree that is planted beside the waters. It stretches out its roots to the stream and reaches them into the water. It has nothing to fear. In a year of draught, it shows no distress. It does not even notice when the scorching heat comes. Its foliage is luxuriant, ever fresh and green. It never stops bearing fruit.

Untouched by any fear, you will not be anxious or full of care. You will make the Lord your refuge. You will live serene and calm and keep on yielding fruit.

Philippians 3:10

Oh, that I may know Him and the power of His resurrection! My determined purpose is that I may progressively become more deeply and intimately acquainted with Him, perceiving, recognizing and understanding the wonders of His Person more strongly and clearly. In that same way, may I come to know the power overflowing from Him and His resurrection and experience personally the mighty power that brought Him back to life again. May I know the power that His coming back to life gives to every believer. Oh, that I might be continuously transformed in spirit into His likeness and that I may attain the spiritual and moral resurrection that lifts me out from the dead, even while I am in the body.

I will be one, who lives in the fresh newness of life. I will be one of those, who are alive from the dead!

John 11:25–27

I AM the Resurrection and the Life! I AM the One, Who raises the dead to life—the One, Who brings people back to life and I AM life itself. If you have faith in Me, if you believe in, adhere to, trust in and rely on Me, although you may die—yet, shall you live. You will come to life again. Whoever continues to live, in Me, shall never actually ever die at all, to all eternity. You are given eternal life for believing in Me. Do you believe this? Is this your faith?

Yes, My Lord, I have believed and I do believe that You are the Christ, the Son of God, the Anointed One, even He, Who was to come into the world. You are the promised Savior, God's Son, Who has come into the world from God. It is for You that the world has waited. I am sure that You are the Messiah—the Expected One.

HOPE

My Beloved—Rest. And again I say, Rest in the beautiful Sabbath Rest I have chosen for you. I plan for you to have a well rounded life—a blessed life, chosen and well planned by Me, full of surprises and delights along the way. I will continually surprise you with My love. You will exclaim with delight and sheer joy "For me?!" as you open each new gift. You, truly, will lack in no good thing. I will bless you first and then a multitude with My message of love, forgiveness, mercy and hope. I will teach My Bride to be full of hope. They will never be hopeless as they come to know, deeply, that with Me, all things are possible. There is nothing too hard for Me. They will have hope in the here and now and hope in the future. No situation, no condition, no possibility will leave them without hope.

In My love for My Bride, I will pour out a double portion of hope, a special measure of hope—blessed hope in the Blessed Hope.

Lamentations 3:21–26

Yet, there is one ray of hope. I still dare to hope. The reason I can still find hope is—the Eternal's love is lasting and will never fail. The unfailing love of the Lord never ends. The favors of Yahweh are not past. His kindnesses are not exhausted. In my mind, I keep returning to something that gives me hope. I call this to mind as my reason to have hope—I have hope and expectation that the Lord's mercy never ends. It is only the Lord's mercies that have kept us from complete destruction. We are not consumed because of His compassion. The Lord can always be trusted to show great mercy and tender compassion.

Great is His faithfulness! Abundant is His stability! His lovingkindness begins afresh each day. His mercies fail not and have no limit. They are new every morning. Hope comes with the dawn.

My soul claims the Lord as my inheritance. My heart whispers,

The Lord is my portion. I will trust Him yet. I will expectantly wait and hope in Him. The Lord is wonderfully good to those, who hopefully and expectantly wait for Him—to those, who seek Him—those, who inquire of Him and require Him by right of necessity and on the authority of His Word.

It is a good thing to hope for help from God, to wait patiently till rescue comes from the Lord. It is good both to hope and wait quietly for the salvation, the safety and the ease of the Lord. The saving help of our Savior will save us.

Deep in my heart, I say to myself, The Lord is all I need. I can depend on Him. I will hope in the Lord!

Isaiah 49:23

Then you will know with understanding, based on and grounded in personal experience—that I AM the Lord. Those, who hope in Me will never be disappointed. Those, who wait for, look for, and expect Me—will not be sorry.

Psalm 147:11

The Lord delights in those, who reverently worship Him and those, who put their hope in His unfailing love. The Lord is pleased with those, who respect Him. The Lord loves those, who trust in His love. The Lord takes pleasure in those, who wait for His grace and lovingkindness. The Lord values those, who fear Him. The Lord is faithful to those, who depend on His faithful care, His mercy and His steadfast love.

Romans 15:4

Whatever was written in the Scriptures, in former days, was written for our instruction that by our steadfast and patient endurance, as we wait for God's promises, we might draw encouragement, comfort and counsel from the Scriptures. We can have and hold fast to and cherish hope, because of all of God's promises in the Scriptures.

Psalm 42:5

Why are you downcast, O my soul? Why so full of heaviness and misery? Why is my inner self so disquieted, despairing, despondent and discouraged within me? Why all these sighs and all this groaning? Why am I so upset?

Put your hope in God, for I shall, yet, praise Him and give Him thanks. I wait expectantly for His saving Presence—my Savior, my Salvation, my Deliverer, my Help, my Hope and my God.

Psalm 130:5

I wait for the Lord. My soul does wait and in His Word, I do hope. I am trusting in the Lord, My whole being is confident and hopes in the Lord. I have faith in His promise. I expectantly wait. I wait for the Lord to help me. I look to the Lord and in Him, I do hope.

I am waiting for You, Lord. I am counting on You. I trust in Your promises. In Your Word, I have hope.

Titus 2:13

We expect the blessed fulfillment of our certain hope. We are awaiting and looking for the happy fulfillment, the realization of our blessed hope, even the glorious splendor of the appearing of our great God and Savior, Christ Jesus, the Messiah, our Deliverer, the Anointed One, Who is the fulfillment of all of our hopes.

Romans 15:13

The Lord, Who inspires all our hope, is the Source of hope, the Giver of hope and the Fountain of hope. May the God of Hope so fill you with all joy and peace in believing, through the experience of your faith that by the power of the Holy Spirit, you may abound and be overflowing, bubbling over with hope! May your whole life and outlook be rich and radiant with hope.

 PRAYERS

Beloved Intercessor—Yes, I will. I hear the prayers of your heart and I say, Yes. I will use you in ways you know not. Yes, I will give you a voice and the right words at the right time. Open your mouth and I will fill it. Trust in Me to speak through you. I will take all of the load of trying to prepare ahead of time, of striving and straining for the right words to say at the right time, to the right people. Be at perfect peace and trust in My promise to never leave or forsake you but to be with you constantly, day and night. Rest in the fact that the burden is not yours but I have taken it from you. Rejoice that you are a chosen, yielded vessel that I can flow through. You will be surprised at what you hear coming from your own mouth and it will bring you great joy as you realize that I have chosen you and I AM using you. Your prayers will be a blessing to others, to impart new life and hope and joy. You will be a living testimony and you will always leave behind My fragrance. You have been heard, recorded and answered and the answer is, Yes!

Beloved, the answer is, Yes and never, No. I have placed the desire in your heart to pray for your needs and the needs of others. Your desire has already been done in Heaven. You can start rejoicing now because all of your prayers have been answered in the affirmative. I affirm and commend your prayers. You are My beloved intercessor and I have appointed you watchman over much. You have been proven faithful and trustworthy with a little and I now set you over much.

The prayers of the saints are a very holy sacrifice and they are very precious to Me. Tell My Beloved for Me that I love them and that the answer is, Yes.

Thank you, for your sweet smelling sacrifice laid on the alter in love. Any offering of time alone with Me will be greatly rewarded. It is the very best investment you can possibly make for your life and for the lives of others, who are lifted in prayer. I promise every prayer is heard and recorded and acted upon. Not one goes unheeded, not one is ever lost. Prayers are much more precious than gold. I accept each one, as a gift of love and commitment, an act of faith and trust and a declaration of hope. Prayer can turn the tide and move mountains. Prayer can turn war into peace and mourning into joy. Prayer makes tremendous power available.

Stop and pray. Come apart to pray. Take time to pray. I will always meet with you and we will have communion, one with another. Prayers are a special gift of love, accepted and received in great love. Come and commune with Me.

Yes, dear one, Yes. The answer is, Yes even before you ask. I AM moving Heaven and earth to answer your prayer, to take care of your every need and to minister to you. I will heal you and keep you fit and ready for service.

I want you to be fit and ready, even more than you want it. Thank you, for working with Me for your healing. Thank you, for listening and obeying. Thank you, for leaning on Me and not on your own understanding. Thank you, for depending on Me and not on the arm of flesh. Thank you, that I AM your Source of information. Thank you, for coming to Me first and not last. I will liberally supply. I will be there for you, day and night. If you seek My wisdom, I will upbraid you not. I commend you for seeking the right Source and turning to Me for your every need. You will be comforted, for I AM the Comforter. You will be strengthened with My strength. You will be helped and healed and well taken care of.

Thank you, for coming to Me. The answer is, Yes!

Matthew 6:9–15

When you pray, pray like this. Let this be how you pray. Father of ours, our Heavenly Father, Who reigns in the Heavens, may Your name be held holy and kept holy. May Your name be revered and honored. Hollowed be Your name. Your Kingdom come. Your Reign begin. May what You want be done. Come and set up Your Kingdom so that everyone on earth will obey You, as You are obeyed in Heaven. Your will be done on earth, as it is in Heaven. Accomplished be Thy will! Give us the bread of life today and tomorrow. Give us our food, our needful daily bread. Forgive us what we owe to You. Forgive us the wrongs we have done, as we forgive those, who have wronged us. Forgive us our debts to You, as we forgive all offenders and offenses. Forgive us, as we forgive all shortcomings and trespasses against us. Forgive us our sins, as we forgive those, who have sinned against us. Let us not be put to the test. Do not allow us to be subject to or yield to temptation. Rescue us from the evil one and from error. Deliver us and protect us from all evil. Keep us safe. For, Yours is the Kingdom and the power and the glory forever! Amen. You are ablaze in beauty, Lord! Keep us forgiven with You and forgiving others. For, if you forgive the failures of others, if you forgive their reckless and willful sins, their trespasses against you, their offenses and all of the wrongs done to you—letting them go entirely, leaving them, giving up all resentment—your Heavenly Father will also forgive your failures and even your faults. But if you don't forgive others, your Father will not forgive you. In prayer there is a connection between what God does and what you do. You can't get forgiveness from God without forgiving others. If you refuse to do your part, you cut yourself off from God's part.

James 5:16

Pray for one another that you may be healed, restored to spiritual wholeness of mind and heart. The earnest, heartfelt, continued prayer of the righteous, makes tremendous power available, dynamic in its working, bringing powerful results.

When a believing person prays, great things happen!

1 Thessalonians 5:16–18

Be happy in your faith. Rejoice and be glad-hearted continually. Always be joyful and never stop praying, whatever happens. Pray regularly. Pray without ceasing. Pray perseveringly—never give up praying. Thank God in everything, no matter what the circumstance may be. Be thankful and give thanks for this is the will of God for you, who are in Christ Jesus, the Revealer and the Mediator of that will. Thank God whatever happens—this is what God wants from you.

Philippians 4:6

Be careful for nothing! Let no care trouble you. Entertain no worry about anything. Don't have anxiety about anything, instead pray. Pray earnestly. Tell God every detail of your needs and all of your desires and don't forget to thank Him for His answers and for all that He has done. Let petitions and praises shape your worries into prayers. It's wonderful what happens when Christ displaces worry in your life. Before you know it, a sense of God's wholeness and trusting everything to come together for good, will come and settle down on you.

In everything, in every situation, under all circumstances with petition and supplication and entreaty, joined with thanksgiving and gratitude, continue to let your requests be, unreservedly, made known to God.

Don't worry, pray. With thankful hearts, offer up your prayers.

Matthew 21:22

You will receive everything you ask for in prayer, no matter what it is, if you have trust. All things, whatsoever, you ask in prayer, in His will, you can rest assured—He will give you. Include absolutely everything from small to large in your, believing, prayer. Lay it before God and have faith that you will receive everything you ask for in prayer. Believe and receive!

Psalm 17:6–8

I pray to You, O God, because You will help me. Listen to and answer my prayer. Give me audience and hear what I have to say, O God! I call on You, my God. I entreat You, give ear to and answer my prayer.

Show me the wonder of Your great love. Your love is wonderful. Show me Your unfailing love in wonderful ways. Show evidence of

Your faithful love. Show me Your marvelous lovingkindness. Make clear Your compassionate love and mercy and wondrous kindness. Show me how marvelous Your true love can be. Display Your faithfulness in wondrous deed. With Your right hand, You deliver those, who seek refuge in You from their assailants and from all of their foes. Your mighty arm protects those, who run to You for safety from their enemies. You are the Savior of all, who put their trust in You. You save all, who seek sanctuary and shelter with You. You are the Savior of those, who hope in Your strength.

Guard and keep me as the apple of Your eye. Keep Your eyes upon me. Protect me as You would the delicate pupil of Your very Own eye. Hide me in the shadow of Your wings.

Psalm 116:1–2

I love the Lord because He has heard my prayer and now hears my voice and my supplication. Because He has inclined His ear to me, I will call upon Him as long as I live. I will entreat Him while life lasts because He pays attention to me and always gives me a hearing. Because He bends down and listens, I will pray as long as I have breath. I am filled with love for Him when Yahweh hears my prayers and answers them.

I love you, Lord. You have answered my prayers.

1 John 5:14–15

This is the confidence we have in approaching God, our fearlessness toward Him consists in this, that if we ask anything, according to His will, He listens to us. We can rest assured that He hears us and that we have the petitions that we desire of Him. We are sure our prayers have already been answered.

Isaiah 65:24

I will answer their prayers before they even call to Me. While they are still talking to Me about their needs, I will go ahead and provide for their needs. While they are still speaking, I will respond. I will help them while they are still asking for help. Even before they finish praying to Me, I will answer.

When you call to Me, when you pray, I will listen and I will hear from Heaven. I will be there at your point of need, in your time of need. Even before you speak, I will hear and answer.

 LIFE

Love of My Life—Yes, you are—I promise you are! You bring such joy and blessing to Me and to My life. I wish you could see with My eyes and realize how very precious you are to Me. Thank you, for being a willing vessel, ready to receive all of the love I have for you and for My beloved Bride who is waiting, longing to receive a love letter from Me. Thank you, for being willing and eager to be My life on earth, to be My hands and My feet and My very heartbeat in the world. Thank you, for allowing Me to live and move and have My being in and through you as I reach out to bless and to love others through you.

Thank you, for realizing how very alive and active My Word, truly, is. Thank you, for having such joy in finding life in the Word. Thank you, for considering it a privilege, an honor, a blessing and a true joy to study and to search and seek in My holy Scriptures. Thank you, for being thrilled by the eternal life flowing out of My holy Word.

Thank you, for giving your very life—your time and laying down all of your plans and hopes and dreams, at this time of your life, to receive, record and research A Long Love Letter *written to My beloved Bride. Thank you, for your precious life laid on the alter of sacrifice that I might live in and through you. Thank you, for the holy offering laid on the alter with love. Thank you, for your gift to Me and to the others that I will reach through you. Thank you, for your love and for choosing Me as the love of your life.*

Look up and live, truly live, in My gift of life and life abundant. I have promised you abundance in every area, from every direction, by all means. I promise fullness of life and prosperity and blessings without number, love abounding and peace eternal and undisturbed. Try to count your blessings and you will see how I have blessed and I AM blessing you. You will look forward, with eager anticipation, to the blessings that are on the way. Each one is a manifestation of My love so that you can actually see, touch, feel, experience and know the reality of My love surrounding you. Walk in the peace of My protection. Sit in the seat of authority. Know that you rule and reign now—not at some future date. I have given you unlimited authority in this present day and time. Lie down and rest in perfect peace, a peace that passes all understanding, a peace that will not be disturbed for all eternity. Rise up rested and refreshed, to live a life that is full and rich—a life that is spilling over with life. Touch those around you with the gift of life—life eternal and perpetually abundant.

John 3:16

For God so greatly loved and dearly prized the world that He gave up His only Son, the Uniquely Begotten One, so that whoever believes in Him might not be lost—shall not perish but have everlasting life.

John 10:10

I came that they may have and enjoy life and have it in abundance. I came that they may have life in all of its fullness, to the full, till it overflows. I came so that they may have real and eternal life—better life than they ever dreamed. I came so they will have everything they need in life, in full measure, over and above measure! I, alone, came in order that they might lay hold of and possess life and that they might possess it superabundantly!

Psalm 36:7–9

How precious is Your steadfast love, O Lord! How exquisite is Your unfailing love and Your faithful care! How excellent is Your lovingkindness, Your grace and Your mercy! Your love is a precious treasure. You protect all humanity under the shadow of Your wings. They seek and take refuge and put their trust in You. They relish and feast on the abundance of Your house. They are refreshed and fully satisfied from your vast resources. They have their fill of the prime and choice gifts of Your house. You cause them to drink from the streams of Your pleasures, Your rivers of delight. With You is the Fountain of Life. Life's own fountain is within Your Presence. You are the Giver of life. The Source of life itself springs from You.

In Your light, we see light. In Your light, we are bathed in light. Your light lets us enjoy life. We shall increase in wisdom as You enlighten us.

Proverbs 19:23

Reverence for the Lord conduces to life. Those who have it will have need of nothing. It brings food and shelter and security. No evil will come their way. They will rest content, untouched by harm or calamity. They will abide unvisited by misfortune.

Those, who respect the Lord will live and be satisfied, unbothered by trouble. Showing respect to the Lord, brings true life. You can relax without fear of danger.

The worshipful fear of the Lord is life itself, a full life, a serene life. He who has it rests secure, protected from all fear of evil.

Joshua 22:5

Take diligent heed to do all the commands and the law. Be very careful to obey the precepts. Be ever mindful to love the Eternal, your God and always to live His life. Follow Him faithfully and walk in all of His ways. Conform to His ways and follow His paths always.

Be faithful to the Lord your God, cling to Him and hold fast to Him. Unite with Yahweh, your God, remain loyal to Him, worship Him and obey Him. Serve the Lord with all of your whole heart and mind and soul—with all of your strength and all of your being, with your very life!

1 Timothy 4:8

Physical training and bodily exercises are of some value but godliness, spiritual training, is useful and of value in everything, in every way and in every respect. Its benefits are without limit. It is of service, in all directions. Spiritual fitness is essential, for it holds promise for the present life and also for the life that is to come. It carries with it a promise of life, both here and hereafter. Training your body helps you in some ways but serving God helps you in every way. It promises life now and forever. Train yourself for life. Live the life, whose goal is God.

John 6:63

It is the Spirit, Who gives life. He is the Life-Giver. The flesh conveys no benefit whatever. There is no value or profit in it. The words and truths that I have been speaking to you are Spirit and life.

Human effort accomplishes nothing. Muscle and willpower don't make anything happen. Every word that I speak to you is a Spirit-Filled word and so it is life making. My words are life.

Deuteronomy 30:19–20

I have set before you life and death, blessing or curse. Oh, that you would choose life—that you and your descendants might live! Oh, that you would love the Lord your God and obey His voice that you would cling to Him and hold fast to Him, for He is your life and your length of days! Love Adonai, pay attention to what He says, stay close to Him, for that is the purpose of your life. Commit yourself to Him. Walk in His ways. Keep His regulations and rules so that you may live, really live, life exuberantly!

Chapter 5

I Will Cherish You

 SINGING

Bride of Mine—I will hold your hand and gently lead you and guide you to walk, then dance down the path I have chosen for you. I rejoice over you with singing and I will lead you to sing a joyful song. I will lead you to know and understand true joy—not the empty, shallow, meaningless laughter of the world but deep and constant joy—the true joy of knowing and understanding My unconditional, everlasting love for you. That knowledge will give you security and peace and a constant portion of joy. Rejoice! And again I say, Rejoice! Dance for joy! Abide in blissful contentment. I love you and I sing a love song to you.

Psalm 66:17

As I called out to the Lord for help, I praised Him with song. When I appealed to Him in words, praise was on the tip of my tongue. I cried out to Him for help, praising Him as I spoke and He answered me. As I called with my mouth, my tongue shaped the sound of music, exulting Him. No sooner had I called out to Him than I was praising Him for answering me.

1 Chronicles 16:8–9

O give thanks to the Lord! Call upon His name. Proclaim His greatness. Make known His doings among the people. Celebrate His exploits among the nations. Let the whole world know what He has done. Tell the people, of the world, of His mighty deeds.

Sing to Him! Sing praises and make music unto Him. Greet Him with song and psalm. Recount His acts of miracles. Tell everyone about all of His wondrous works and devoutly praise Him.

Ephesians 5:19

Ever be filled with the Spirit. Speak to one another, reciting psalms and hymns and spiritual songs, as you praise the Lord with all of your heart. Express your joy in singing among yourselves. Make melody with the music of your hearts to the Lord!

Colossians 3:16

Let the Word, in all of its richness, find a home with you. Let Christ's teachings live in your hearts, making you rich in true wisdom. Use psalms and hymns and spiritual songs to teach and instruct one another. Sing them out, singing with grace in your hearts to the Lord, with gratitude rising into song.

Psalm 89:1–2

I will sing of the Lord's great love forever. With my mouth will I make known Your faithfulness, from generation to generation, through all generations. Anyone yet to be born will hear me praise Your faithfulness—young and old will hear about Your blessings!

I will declare that Your love stands firm forever. I will proclaim that You have established Your faithfulness in Heaven itself. Your faithfulness have You established unchangeable and perpetual. I will keep singing of the tender mercies and the lovingkindness of the Lord forever. I'll tell them, God's love can always be trusted. His steadfast love is confirmed forever.

Your love, O God, is my song and I will sing it! I'll never quit telling the story of Your great love.

Psalm 105:43

He brought forth His people with joy and great gladness and singing. With exultant shoutings, with shouts of triumph, He led His chosen ones. They celebrated with rejoicing, singing joyous songs.

Psalm 147:1

Hallelujah! Praise the Lord! It is good to sing praises to our God. A hymn of praise is seemly. It is pleasant to make melody and be thankful to our God. It is good and right to chant psalms and sing glorious praise. It is a joyful thing to honor our gracious God with sweet praises in song.

Psalm 104:33–34

I will sing to the Lord as long as I live. I will sing praise to my God while I have my being. I will make music for my God. I will sing to Yahweh. Yes, I will touch the strings to my God. All of my life, I will be glad in the Lord. My gladness comes from Him. I am happy in the Lord.

I am so pleased to be singing to God. Oh, let me sing hymns to my God as long as I live! Let my song please Him. My meditation of the Lord shall be sweet. May my meditation be sweet to Him.

May this prayer find acceptance with Him. May He be pleased with all of these thoughts of Him.

I will rejoice in Jehovah. He is the Source of all my joy. I will sing praise to the Eternal while I have breath. I will praise my God to my last breath.

Isaiah 54:1–5

Sing O barren one! You, who have never been in labor or travailed with child. O barren soul, who never bore, sing songs! Break into song O childless one! Burst into jubilant song! Break forth into singing with cries of joy and gladness! Shout in triumph, you, who have never been with child for the spiritual children of the desolate one will be more than the children of the married wife, says the Lord. More numerous are the children of the single than the married. More are the children of the forsaken, deserted wife than the beloved of her husband, who lives in wedlock.

For your Maker, your Creator is your husband. Yahweh Saboath, the Lord of Armies is He, Who takes up your cause. The Lord of Hosts, your Defender will rescue you. The Holy One of Israel is your Redeemer. Your Ransomer is the Holy One. The Lord Almighty will save you. The Lord All-Powerful is your Savior. The God of the whole earth is your Bridegroom.

Psalm 42:8

The Lord will command His lovingkindness in the daytime and in the night His song will be with me. God promises to love me all day and sing songs to me all through the night. The Lord shows His constant love everyday. Throughout the day, God pours His unfailing love upon me. By day, He bestows His grace and confirms His steadfast, faithful love.

In the night season, I will sing songs of Him. All through the night I will sing to Him and pray to my living God, the God of my life, Who gives me life.

Zephaniah 3:17

The Lord, your God, has arrived to live among you. Adonai is right there in the midst of you. He is a Mighty One—a Savior, Who saves! He is a victorious Savior, a Warrior, Who gives victory and wins victory after victory. He will always be with you. The Mighty One will save you. He is a hero, Who saves. He will exult over you with shouts of triumph. He will rejoice over you with joy and great gladness.

Yahweh will renew you in His love. He will refresh your life with His love. He will make you to rejoice with gladness. He will calm all of your fears. He will quiet you and soothe you with His love. He will love you and not accuse you. He will rest in silent satisfaction and in His love, He will be silent and make no mention of past sins or even recall them. He will rejoice over you with singing. He celebrates and sings because of you. Yahweh, your God is there with you—the Warrior Savior. He will dance with shouts of jubilation, for you, as on a day of festival. He will rejoice over you with joy. Is that a joyous choir I hear? No, it is the Lord, Himself, exulting over you by singing a happy song.

Song of Songs 2:10–13

My Beloved sings and calls to me. I can hear my true love calling, Arise! Rise up My love, My fair one and come away with Me. For behold, the winter is past, the rain is over and gone. The flowers appear on the earth. Lilacs are exuberantly purple and perfumed, cherry trees are fragrant with blossoms. The air is fragrant with blossoming vines. The time of the spring song has come. The whole world is a choir and singing! The season of the glad song has come. The voice of the turtledove is heard in our land. The doves cooing note is heard. The time for singing has come. Come then My gentle dove, My dear friend, My beautiful one. Come to Me. Come away with Me.

 JOY

Joy of My Heart—My message to you is to rest and rejoice. Learn and experience true merriment of the soul. Learn the healing effects of joy and rejoicing. Truly, a merry heart does good, better than any medicine. Bring a sacrifice of joy and watch it multiply into a rich and abundant harvest of rejoicing. Reap a harvest of rejoicing from a cup of joy scattered and broadcast in the fertile field of sad and frightened souls around you. The joy of the Lord is your strength and at the same time your buckler and shield. This is the day I have created for you to rejoice and be glad. Rejoice! And again I say, Rejoice! I love you and there is nothing to fear.

You will see what a beautiful gift joy is. My gift of joy will never leave you. It has come to stay. I have given you a double portion of joy, enough to keep, to share and to give away, an overflowing abundance. My joy will radiate out from you like a healing balm, anointing everyone who comes near. As you share with others, you will see the healing effect of joy manifest before your very eyes when the weight is lifted and they grow in strength. You will see their countenance change, from sad and forlorn and hopeless, to smiling with new hope and new life. You will see loving gratitude spring forth as the new hope and strength take root. I will bless you with the visible evidence, of the healing power, of joy. You will behold the miracle of joy as I transform weakened and sad ones into smiling, strong, healthy and joyful souls before your eyes. You will know and understand and witness the gift you have shared and the healing effect of joy.

My will for you is joy, even a constant portion of true joy. As you look with eyes of faith, you will see beyond any current problems to the victory beyond and you will anticipate the outcome with joy. I never said there would never be any problems but I did promise you victory every time, in all things, in all ways and by all means! Walking by faith is very important for keeping your constant portion of joy. Your spiritual eyes will be fixed and fastened on the victorious, joyous outcome. Great faith starts rejoicing ahead of time, knowing the great gladness that lies ahead.

Wherever you go, you will take My peace and leave behind joy. In a world hurrying to nowhere, your slow, easy pace will be a refreshing and healing. Even though a lot will be accomplished, you will do it slowly and peacefully. Notice your times of greatest joy. They are in times of rest and peace and quiet. I don't plan for you to live a hurried, harried life like so many, filling their lives with noise and business and meaninglessness. I have planned for you to live a set apart, holy life of peace and quiet and great and abiding joy—true joy that bubbles up from deep inside and spills over on all who come near—a contagious joy that is a gift from Me. Joy is a refreshing from all of the cares of life. Joy is a holy laughter that heals and binds up wounds and hurts, that binds together in love and speaks volumes of love.

Rejoice and receive My gift of great and abiding joy.
Live each day in gladness and joy, a very special gift of
My great love for you.

Proverbs 17:22

A joyful heart is good medicine.
A happy heart works an excellent cure.
A glad heart is an excellent remedy.
A cheerful heart makes for a quick recovery.
A cheerful mind works healing.
A cheerful disposition is good for your health.
A rejoicing heart does good to the whole body.
A merry heart makes a cheerful countenance.
If you are cheerful, you feel good.

Proverbs 15:15

Those, who have a glad heart, have a continual feast, regardless of the circumstances. Those, whose heart is happy, have an unending banquet. Those, who are of a merry heart, have contentment and continual tranquility. Contentment is a feast without end. A cheerful heart brings a smile to your face. For the joyous heart, it is always festival time.

Philippians 4:4

Rejoice in the Lord, always. Again I say, Rejoice. Delight and gladden yourselves in Him. All joy be yours, at all times, in your union with the Lord. With the help of the Lord, always keep a glad spirit. Be happy and celebrate God—revel in Him. Never lose your Christian joy. Let me say it again, Never lose it! Find your joy in the Lord at all times. Always be full of the joy of the Lord.

James 1:2–4

Rejoice! Consider it, wholly, joyful. Greet it as nothing but pure joy. Consider it a matter of unadulterated joy without any mixture of sorrow—whenever, you are enveloped in many kinds of trouble and temptation. When you meet with any sort of trial, let it be an opportunity for joy. Whenever trouble comes your way, you should look upon this as the very source of extreme joy, while being aware at the same time that the very genuineness of your faith creates the power to endure. When your faith is tested, your endurance has a chance to grow. So, let it grow! Let endurance have its perfection, for when your endurance is fully developed, you will be strong in character and ready for anything.

Be assured and understand that in the testing of your faith, that very trial and proving, leads to and produces, develops and brings out, endurance, steadfastness and fortitude. When you are tested in different ways, faith having been tested, for the purpose of being approved and having met the test, brings out patience that does not lose heart or courage under trials. When troubles test your faith and your faith has passed through the ordeal of testing, the result is the ability to pass the breaking point and not to break.

Let endurance, steadfastness and patience have full play and do a perfect work, a thorough finished work, so that you may be perfectly and fully developed, spiritually mature and complete, whole and finished in every detail and perfectly equipped with no defects, not coming short, lacking in nothing, without even a single weak spot. You won't need anything. You will have everything you need.

Consider it a sheer gift when challenges come at you from all sides. You know that under pressure your faith is forced into the open and into action and shows its true colors. So don't try to get out of anything prematurely. Let it do its work so that you become mature, completed and perfected, not deficient in any way.

Habakkuk 3:18–19

I celebrate because the Lord saves me! I rejoice in God my Savior! I will exult in the victorious God of my salvation! I take joy in the God of my deliverance—my saving God. God is my strength, my personal bravery and my invincible army.

The Lord will guide my feet to the end that I may triumph with His song. He makes my feet like hind's feet and will make me to walk, not stand in terror, but walk and make spiritual progress upon my high places—the mountains of trouble, suffering and responsibility. He makes me like a deer that does not stumble so that I can walk on the steep mountains. He makes me swift and surefooted as a deer and enables me to stride over my high places.

You make my feet as light as a doe's and You let me stride upon the heights, O God!

Psalm 5:11

Lord, You bless the uncompromisingly righteous. You bless all, who are upright and in right standing with You. Let all, who take refuge and put their trust in You, rejoice! Let them ever sing glad songs and shout and leap for joy, for You shelter, protect, defend and strengthen all those, who love Your name. Let them ever sing for joy!

Psalm 118:24

This is the day which the Lord has brought about, we will rejoice and be glad in it! Today let us celebrate and be festive with joy. This is a day we owe to the Eternal. Let us exult in Him!

Nehemiah 8:10

This day is holy to our Lord. This is a sacred day, consecrated to God. Don't be grieved or depressed or dejected. Do not be saddened or downcast, for this day is a day of joy unto the Lord. Let there be no sadness, for the joy of the Lord is your strength. The joy of Jehovah is your refuge and your stronghold. This is a special day for Yahweh and He will make you happy and strong. Your rejoicing, in the Lord, is the source of your strength.

Psalm 16:11

You reveal to me and show me the path of life. You teach me how to live a holy life. In Your Presence is fullness of pure joy. I'm happy from the inside out. Being with You fills me with abounding joy. Being near You makes me glad. Sitting by Your side, I will always be joyful—at Your right hand are pleasures and delights forevermore.

Ever since You took my hand, I'm walking the right way. You've got my feet on the right path of life. You have let me experience the complete, perfect joy of life—the exquisite, everlasting pleasure of Your Own eternal Presence. Imagine the pleasures of living with You forever!

Psalm 30:11–12

You have turned my mourning into joyful dancing for me. You have changed my sobbing into a whirling dance. You have turned my heaviness into gladness. You took away my clothes of sadness and clothed me in happiness. You have stripped off my sackcloth and clothed me with joy. You tore off my black band of mourning and decked me with wildflowers. You have turned my lamenting into a processional. No longer am I sad. You have taken my sorrow and surrounded me with joy.

O Lord, my God, I will give thanks to You forever. I thank You, with all of my heart. My whole being will sing hymns of praise to You unceasingly. My soul will never cease to praise You. My heart will never tire of, joyfully, singing praises to You. I will not be silent—I can't keep quiet about You, Yahweh, my God. I will praise You and thank You, forever!

1 Peter 1:8

Without having seen Him, you love Him. Though you do not even now see Him, You believe and trust and have faith in Him. You exult and thrill with inexpressible and glorious, triumphant heavenly joy! You are happy with laughter and singing. You are filled with the joy, full of glory, that comes from Heaven itself.

 PRECIOUS

Precious Love—I will be close, healing and restoring, rejuvenating and replenishing. I will, I promise, keep you young and healthy. I will renew your youth like the eagle. People will be more and more surprised at your countenance as you draw closer to Me. Rejoice and be exceedingly glad, the aura others see and comment on will be a manifestation of My Presence within you. They will be drawn to My Presence and gather up the overflow and turn to Me as the Source.

If you knew how precious you were to Me, you could not stop smiling. You would have such joy bubbling up within you—you would dance for pure joy. The joy, deep within you, would be spilling over into dancing feet.

Precious Loved One, precious are these days when you have come apart from the world and entered into your prayer closet and shut the door. There are so few that make the sacrifice of laying down their lives and all of their plans to come away with Me. Precious is our time, alone, together. Precious is our love. Precious is sharing our hearts with one another with no limit of time when I can freely commune with you day and night. Precious is your heart full of love for your Bridegroom. Precious is your listening ear, longing to hear the voice of your Beloved. Precious are your eyes, turned from the world and all others toward Me. I will see that you see Me—I will reveal Myself to you.

I love you. You are valued and very precious to Me.

Psalm 103:5

The Lord satisfies me with good as long as I live. He fills my lifetime with good things. He wraps me in goodness and eternal beauty. He gives me all my heart's desire. He fills my life with blessings so that I become young again. He renews my youth, I'm always young in His Presence. Each day that we live, He provides for our needs and gives us strength. He renews our youth like the eagle—strong, overcoming and soaring.

Isaiah 40:28–31

Have you not heard? Have you not known? The everlasting God, the Lord forever, Yahweh, the Creator of all that you can see, does not grow weary. He does not become tired or need to rest. He does not even pause to catch His breath. He never becomes faint or feeble. He knows everything. His knowledge is beyond all thinking. His wisdom cannot be measured. His discernment is beyond scrutiny. His insight is unfathomable. His understanding is unsearchable.

He energizes those, who get tired. He invigorates the exhausted. He gives new vigor to the weak. To those, who have no might, He increases strength. He gives fresh spirit to the spent. He gives power to the powerless causing it to multiply and making it abound.

Youth itself may weaken and the warrior may faint and flag in zeal but those, who trust in the Lord will find new strength and never tire. Even young men in their prime may collapse and fall. The fittest may helplessly stumble and utterly fall prostrate but those who put their hope in Yahweh will regain their strength. Those, who depend on the Lord for help, will find their strength renewed.

Those, who wait for the Lord—those who look to the Eternal and expect and hope in Him—those, who trust in Adonai shall become strong again. They will find new strength. Those expecting Jehovah pass to power.

They will soar aloft as with eagle's wings and mount up close to God as eagles mount up to the sun. They will be strong like eagles. They will ascend, soaring upward like eagles in flight.

The will run and never be tired. They will walk and not become weary. They will march on and not need to rest.

1 Peter 2:4

Come to Him, that Living, Life-Giving Stone. He is the Stone rejected and thrown away by men but chosen and very precious in God's sight. Come to Christ, the Chief Cornerstone of God's temple. Everything will be built on this important and precious

Rock. Come and like living stones, be built into a spiritual house for a holy, dedicated, consecrated priesthood, who will offer up those spiritual sacrifices that are acceptable and pleasing to God through Jesus Christ.

For, thus, it stands in Scripture, Behold, I AM laying in Zion a chosen, honored, valued and very precious Cornerstone. Those, who believe in Him, who adhere to, trust in, and rely on Him shall never be disappointed or put to shame.

To you, who believe, belongs the preciousness. Believers feel His great worth, His preciousness. He is very precious to you, who believe.

Present yourselves as building stones for the construction of a sanctuary, vibrant with life, in which you will serve as holy priests offering Christ-approved lives up to God.

Isaiah 43:4

You are so precious in My sight! I regard you as precious. You are prized and valued in My eyes. Because you are precious and glorious in My sight, I give you honor. You are dearly loved by Me. To Me, you are very dear. You are My Beloved and I love you.

 JEWEL

Jewel of My Kingdom—You are a lovely jewel, sparkling and giving luster and beauty to My Kingdom. I will shine through you and bless My Chosen Ones as you go where I send you in the earth. Through no effort of your own, you will take My Presence with you and be a blessing to those round about you. I have chosen you not because of your ability or success but because of your beautiful, clear, yielded spirit that I can shine through. You don't have to earn My Presence or try to keep it from slipping away by

doing mighty deeds and exploits. It will be a totally effortless achievement on your part as you welcome My Spirit moving and having Its Being and freedom, in and through you.

Thank you, for learning and for deeply knowing the true beauty, the everlasting, eternal, radiant beauty of My Holy Spirit shining out from you and dazzling others with the light of My Presence. You need not be concerned what you will wear or how you will look. Your acceptance comes from Me and not from others. Others will be drawn to you because of My Presence drawing and wooing them to eternal life. Truly, you are a jewel and a precious and priceless gem of My Kingdom.

Beloved, I appreciate your quiet and teachable spirit. Thank you, for being that yielded vessel that I need, so much, in this last day. You see, I need you as you need Me. It is a mutual agreement to work in the harvest fields. We are co-laborers in our labor of love. Just wait until you see what I have planned for you in this Last Great Harvest! Keep your eyes fixed and fastened on Me and you will see My wondrous plan unfold before your wondering eyes, as you rest in Me and wait on Me. I will use you in ways you cannot conceive or imagine or even dream. I have prepared you for such a time as this and I promise you great joy in this time of fulfillment. Be not anxious or dismayed. Trust in Me. I have a plan.

Merely be that beautiful jewel reflecting Me with a gentle, quiet and yielded spirit that will allow Me to shine forth from you in all directions—Bride of Mine, Jewel of My Kingdom.

Ephesians 3:20

Glory be to God! Glory belongs to God, Whose power is at work in us. By His mighty power working within us, He is able to carry out His purpose and accomplish exceedingly, super abundantly, far over and above, infinitely beyond, immeasurably, surpassingly more than we can conceive or think—more than all our highest prayers or desires—more than all our hopes and dreams—more than we would ever dare to ask. What He does goes beyond every expectation!

2 Timothy 2:21

Those who make themselves clean will be used for special purposes. They are dedicated to the Master. Their lives will be holy and pleasing to their Master. They are ready to be used for His good purpose.

If you purge and purify yourself from whatever is ignoble and unclean and separate yourself from contaminating and corrupting influences—if you sever yourself from these things, then you will be set-apart and sanctified, worthy for the Master's use. Stop associating with dishonorable people and you will be honored. By avoiding contact with what has no value, you will be a vessel that is valued. In a state of permanent separation, you will be a highly prized vessel, made holy and ready for the Master's service. You will be a vessel equipped, prepared and useful for honorable and noble purposes. You will be fit and ready for every good work and service of every sort.

Be the kind of vessel God can use!

2 Corinthians 4:6–7

Scripture says, God said, Let there be light! Out of the darkness light shall shine! Let there be light shining in the darkness!

God has caused His light to shine within us, flooding our hearts with His light. He has given us the light of revelation. We are enlightened, illuminated with the knowledge of the majesty and glory of God, as it is manifested in the person and revealed in the face of Jesus Christ, the Messiah. God has shone in our hearts for the spreading abroad of the light that we might make known His glory as it is seen in Christ

The light that now shines within us is held in perishable containers. Everyone can see that the precious treasure of the divine light of the Gospel is from God and not from us. We are a reflection of the light. God is the Source. We are like clay vessels in which precious treasure is stored. Our frail human vessels of earth possess within them the grandeur and the exceeding greatness of the all-surpassing power of the Good News that comes from God alone. This makes it clear that the supreme power belongs to God and does not have its source in us.

Malachi 3:17

The Lord of Hosts says, My people are precious to Me. They belong to Me. They are My very Own. In the day when I compose and prepare My treasure, My Own prized special possession, I will publicly recognize and openly declare them to be My jewels, says Yahweh. When I come to bring justice I will claim them as My Own special people, My Own peculiar treasure. I will protect them and show mercy to them. I will deal tenderly with them and have compassion on them as parents spare their own obedient, dutiful child.

Isaiah 61:10

I will greatly rejoice in the Lord my God, for He has clothed me with garments of salvation. He has covered me with a robe of righteousness. My whole being exults in My God for He has wrapped me in a cloak of integrity and goodness and arrayed me in a garment of triumphant victory. His saving power and justice are the very clothes I wear. They are more beautiful than the jewels worn by a bride and groom.

Isaiah 62:3

You will be so beautiful and prosperous, you will be thought of as a crown of glory and honor in the hand of the Lord. You will be a stunning crown of splendor in the palm of Yahweh's hand. You will be an exceedingly beautiful royal diadem carried by your God. He will hold you aloft for all to see. You will be a jeweled, gold cup held high in the hand of your God.

FAVORITE

Highly Favored One—Blessed be the day of My visitation and this is that day! Bask in My love. Rejoice in My everlasting, unconditional love. Dwell in perfect peace. Know that I have provided for every need and want and desire. Live in a constant state of joy, knowing that all things are working together for your good. Have faith and anticipate, with gladness, all of the good that I have planned for you that is on the way, even now. I promise you showers of blessings, too many to begin to count. I will give you My favor and favor in every situation. You will feel that you surely must be My very favorite as I favor you in all conditions and situations, at all times, in all places.

My favor, in all areas, is a manifestation of My love and My tender, loving care. If you don't realize My favor every time, just wait expectantly and it will soon be revealed to you that, truly, all things are working together for your good. You will come to know and deeply under-

stand that you do live constantly in My favor and My abiding love and care, My Chosen, My Bride, My Favorite.

Psalm 30:5

God's favor is for a lifetime and in His favor is life! There is a lifetime in God's good pleasure and when He is pleased, there is life, abundant! For a lifetime there is only love and goodwill and in His love and goodwill, there is life, indeed!

Psalm 84:11

The Lord God is a Sun to enlighten and a Shield to protect us. The Lord bestows present grace and favor and future glory, honor, splendor and heavenly bliss! No good thing will He withhold from those who walk uprightly.

Yahweh is our Supply and our Helper. He does not withhold prosperity from those, who live blamelessly. For the innocent, He will never refuse His bounty.

God, the Eternal, is our light and a towering protector. He does not hold back any blessing—He never denies blessing or withholds what is good from those, whose lives are pure. Sovereign is God—generous in gifts and glory!

John 1:16

Out of His fullness and abundance, we have all received and all have a share. We were all supplied with one grace after another, with spiritual blessing upon spiritual blessing and even favor upon favor. Each of us has received one gift after another, gift heaped upon gift, gift after gift of love—love following upon love!

Proverbs 22:1

A good name is, rather, to be chosen than great riches and loving favor, rather, than silver and gold. A good reputation is a better choice than great wealth and riches. To be well thought of, to be held in high esteem and to be respected is better than money in the bank. To be loved, with favor, is beyond all treasure.

Isaiah 61:1–3

The Spirit of the Lord is upon me. The Lord has sent me to publish glad tidings—to bring messages of joy, instead of doom and gloom. The Lord has chosen me and sent me to tell, the oppressed, the Good News. He has consecrated me and qualified me to preach the Gospel. He has anointed me to bring the Glad News to the suffering and afflicted. He has sent me as a herald of joy to the humble.

The Lord has sent me to provide for all who grieve. He has sent me to comfort the brokenhearted, to bind up and heal the wounded and to open the eyes of the blind. He has sent me to proclaim liberty to the physical and spiritual captives—to proclaim liberty to all who are bound—to let out into the light, those bound in darkness—to tell the prisoners they are released. They are free!

The Lord has sent me to announce that the time of God's favor has come. A day of vindication by our God has arrived. The day of the salvation of our God is here—a time of grace and pardon, acceptance and great favor.

The Lord has sent me to grant consolation and comfort to all who mourn—to give them a garland of flowers in place of sorrow—the oil of joy and gladness instead of grief—festive ointment instead of tears and beauty for ashes. They will be gaily clad in garments expressive of praise—a glorious mantle of praise instead of the spirit of dejection and despondency—a robe of righteousness instead of a spirit of heaviness—a cloak of joyous praise in place of broken hearts.

They will be called Oaks of Righteousness, lofty, strong and magnificent. They will be called Trees of Victory, Trees of Justice and Trees of Goodness—planted by the Lord for His honor and glory—the Plantings of the Lord that He may be glorified.

2 Corinthians 6:2

The Lord says, In the time of My favor, I have listened to you. In the time of My assured welcome, I have heeded your call. I have harkened to you. I ran to your cry and brought you aid. I have heard you and answered your prayer.

Here is the time of pardon. The day of deliverance has dawned. I have succored you and helped you. Behold, now is the time for a glad and gracious welcome! The hour of My favor has now come! This is the day of salvation!

Indeed, this is God's acceptable time, for His acceptance. This is the hour to receive God's favor. Today is the day for you to be saved. Don't put it off. The time has come. The right time is now. It is here!

Psalm 5:12

Let all who cherish Your name be strengthened by You, Lord, for You dwell among us.

You, Lord, bless the righteous with favor. Like a large shield, You surround us with Your favor. You encompass us with an all-covering shield. You cover us with an armor of favor, shielding us safe. You protect us with your love. You welcome us with open arms when we run to you for cover.

1 Corinthians 16:23

May God's grace and favor rest upon you. May the spiritual blessings of the Lord Jesus Christ be with you. May the goodwill and kindness of the Lord be yours. May the Lord Jesus love you.

Our Lord has His arms open wide for you!

 HEART

Heart of My Heart—You are well prepared for the task at hand and the most important ingredient is your heart. Thank you, for a heart that seeks and finds Me. Thank you, for a heart that pants after Me as the hart pants after streams of fresh water. Thank you, for your heart turned to Me first and foremost—a heart that follows after Me with all of your heart. The world looks on the outward appearance but I look on the heart and yours brings Me great joy. Thank you, for being My heartbeat in the earth. Thank you, for being My hands and My feet but most of all for being My heart and allowing Me to reach out in love to those round about you. The greatest is love. Thank you, for your heart filled with compassion and caring, a heart that breaks for others. I have seen the tears of your heart and they are very precious to Me.

I treasure your heart, aching in true repentance. I cherish your heart that aches to be righteous and in right standing with Me—a heart that loves and cares enough to try to change into My image and likeness. I see your heart that beats for Me, alone. Thank you, that I AM your true heartbeat.

Beloved, I see your grateful heart and it opens the way for Me to pour more blessings upon you. Those, who don't stop and look up and thank Me and appreciate the gifts but even more the Giver of the gifts, stop the flow of blessing. If only, they knew the cost of getting their eyes on the gift and not the Giver of the gift—they would stop and look up and thank Me. I long to lavish My Beloved with every good and perfect gift. I have such wondrous gifts to give, if only they will keep the channel of blessing open. I will always quickly reopen the channel, if they will only turn their eyes upon the Giver and not the gift. So many stumble over this and slide from grace when there are such beautiful packages filled with amazing gifts and delightful surprises awaiting them. I AM a jealous lover and I share My glory and the praise and gratitude due Me with no person or thing. A thankful, grateful heart is the longing of My heart. It is your gift of love for Me.

Love is the gift that keeps on giving. Love is the true gift—the gift of gifts. Give from a generous, giving heart. Give freely with no strings attached, with no charge or cost of any kind. Give and it shall be given unto you—pressed down, shaken together and running over will gifts be returned and given unto you, in many different forms and ways, from all directions. It is impossible to outgive Me—but I appreciate your trying.

Receive My love in such a vast portion that it will spill over and splash over on all, who come near. I AM your Source of love and it is a constant and unending supply. There is no end to My love. The more you give away—the more you receive. So be lavish with My love. Be generous to one and all. Don't hold back. Don't ration it. Don't partial it out but give and give and give again and receive and

*receive and receive again. There is enough for all. There is
an abundant and an everlasting supply.*

*Thank you, for taking the time to listen to My heart's
desire for you and for My beautiful Bride. My heart longs
to impart My wisdom and share My love with My Beloved.
Tell them for Me that I love them—with all of My heart.*

Psalm 42:1–2

As the hart pants and longs for the water brooks and running
streams of cool water, so I pant and long for You, O God. I, truly,
thirst for You, my God. My soul is dry for need of God, the God
of Life. My inner self longs for the living God. Will I ever drink in
God's Presence? When shall I enter into the Presence of God and
behold the face of God?

James 1:17

All good giving and every perfect present, every highly valued
benefit and every beneficial, worthwhile gift comes from above,
descending from the Creator of all light, the Father of the heavenly luminaries. He does not change or even cast a shadow of
change in movement like the sun and the moon. He is a stranger
to change and does not even cast a shifting shadow by motion of
change.

Whatever is good and perfect comes to us from God above,
the Heavenly Father. In His goodness, He chose to make us His
Own by giving us His true Word and we out of all creation have
become His choice possession. He wanted us to be His Own special people, so He sent the true Message to give us new birth that
we might become most important of all of the things He made.

Luke 6:38

Give and gifts will be given to you. Gifts will be yours in full measure—shaken together, pressed down and packed down to make room for more. Gifts brimming over and overflowing will be poured into the pouch formed by your robe and used as a bag to catch all you can hold. Give to others and God will give to you. With the same measure you use to confer benefits on others, it will be measured back to you. The standard you use for others will be applied to you. The way you treat others is the way you will be treated. Give away your life and you will find life given back with bonus and blessing.

Ezekiel 11:20–21

I will give them one heart, a single purpose, singleness and unity of heart. I will give them a new heart and a new mind. I will put a new spirit within them. I will take the stony, unnaturally hardened heart out of their flesh and I will give them a heart of flesh, sensitive and responsive to the touch of their God. I will give them a new nature. I will remove their hard nature and give them a nature that can be touched.

I will take away their stubbornness and make them eager to be completely faithful to Me. I will give them a desire to respect Me completely. I will put inside them a new way of thinking. I will take out their disobedient heart of stone and give them an obedient, tender heart instead. Then they will live by My rules and regulations. They will want to obey Me and faithfully keep all of My commands. They will respect My judgments and put them into practice. They will live according to My statutes and observe and carry out My ordinances. They will obey My orders and keep My laws. They will be My very Own people and I will be their God.

Isaiah 57:15

Thus says Jehovah, the Exalted One, the Majestic One, the High and Lofty One, Who inhabits eternity, Who lives forever, Whose name is Holy—I dwell in the high and holy place in holiness but also with those, who are of a thoroughly penitent heart and a humble spirit that is bruised with sorrow for sin. I renew, revive and refresh the lowly spirit and give new courage to broken, crushed, repentant hearts. Our holy God lives forever in the highest heavens and this is what He says—Though I live high above in the holy place, I AM here to help all, who look to Me and depend on Me. I will be with all, who trust in Me with all of their heart.

Psalm 34:18

The Lord is near to those, who are of a broken heart. He is close to and saves those, who are crushed with sorrow for sin and are humbly and thoroughly penitent. The Lord is there to rescue all, who are discouraged and have given up hope.

Psalm 147:3

The Lord is the Healer of the broken heart. He heals the brokenhearted and binds up their wounds, curing their pain and relieving their sorrows.

The Lord is the Physician for the broken in heart. He renews our hopes and heals our bodies.

1 Corinthians 2:9

It is written, Scripture says, What eye has not seen and ear has not heard and has not entered into the heart, things beyond our imagining, that no human heart has ever conceived—all that, God has prepared and keeps ready for those, who love Him with all their heart—those, who hold Him in affectionate reverence, promptly obeying Him and gratefully recognizing the benefits and blessings He has bestowed.

2 Chronicles 16:9

The eyes of the Lord run, to and fro, throughout the whole earth to show Himself strong in behalf of those, whose hearts are blameless toward Him. The eyes of the Lord search the whole earth in order to strengthen those, whose hearts are fully committed to Him, so that He can show His great power in helping them. The eyes of the Lord go this way and that, flashing back and forth over the whole wide earth, letting it be seen that He is the strong support of those, whose hearts are true to Him. God is always on the alert, constantly on the lookout to bring aid and comfort to those, whose hearts are loyal to Him, hearts full of integrity toward Him, hearts that have utter faith in Him, hearts that are wholeheartedly with Him.

Psalm 119:10–11

With my whole heart have I sought You, inquiring of You and yearning for You. O let me not wander or step aside, either in ignorance or willfully, from Your commandments. Your Word have I hidden in my heart that I might not sin against you.

I have turned to You with all my heart. I have taken Your words to heart. I have treasured Your promises in my heart. Let me not walk away from Your commands. I have stored up and keep in my heart, Your Word. Let me not sin against You!

2 Corinthians 1:22

Whatever God has promised gets stamped with the Yes of Jesus. He has stamped us with His eternal pledge putting His Yes within us.

It is God, Who marked us as His very Own. He has given us the Holy Spirit in our hearts as a foretaste of all that is to come. He has put His brand on us, His mark of ownership. He has given us the Holy Spirit in our hearts as a guarantee that we belong to Him and as the first installment of all that He is going to give us.

God has anointed me and stamped me with His seal and given me the Holy Spirit in my heart as His pledge of future blessings and rewards, a promise of what is to come. The Holy Spirit in my heart is a security deposit, a guarantee of the fulfillment of His promises, a down payment, guaranteeing the full payment—a sure beginning of what He is destined to complete.

Romans 5:5

We know how dearly God loves us and we feel this warm love everywhere within us because God has given us the Holy Spirit to fill our hearts with His love. God's love is poured out and floods our hearts. His love is shed abroad through the Holy Spirit, which has been given to us.

1 Chronicles 16:10–11

Glory in His holy name, triumph in that hallowed name! Celebrate and worship His holy name with all of your heart! Let the hearts of those, who seek the Lord rejoice. Joyful be the hearts of those, who long for the Lord!

Seek the Lord and His strength, keep on searching. Yearn for His face. Untiringly persevere to be in His Presence continually. Constantly, evermore, court His Presence!

Isaiah 40:11

He tends His flock like a shepherd. He gathers the lambs in His arms and carries them close to His heart.

UNCONDITIONAL

Precious Love—I don't condemn you or try to fill you with shame. I support you and encourage you and commend you. Rejoice in My approval and love. I AM proud of you. Your love for Me is My joy. As I look, to and fro, over the earth, I see you and your faithful love and I rejoice. You can do nothing greater, to show your love for Me than to be a yielded vessel that I can move through. I have used your yielded spirit more than you realize. I use you most of all when you don't even know it. Rejoice, evermore, in My love. Rest, totally rest, in My approval of you. Nothing you could possibly do for Me would make Me love you more. My love is a constant not a variable. It is, truly, unconditional and eternal. It is not like human love that so often requires proving and striving to attain and fear that it will slip away. Rest and rejoice in My love that has no conditions.

Yes, beloved Bride, this is why I have chosen you—you are utterly faithful, completely and totally yielded and so eager to receive and share with others what I have revealed to you. You share with humility and wonder that I have chosen you. I need not fear or even be concerned about your trustworthiness and faithfulness. Long ago you proved your perfect love so that I would never doubt your unfailing, eternal love. Just as My love is unconditional, so is yours. You never blame Me when things don't happen the way you have planned. You immediately release your plan to Me and say and mean with all of your heart, "God has a plan! I may not understand it now but He is trustworthy and He is working all things to My good. His plan is better."

Thank you, for entrusting all of your hopes and dreams and plans to Me. I will greatly reward you, precious Bride, for your unfailing love. Love covers a multitude of sins and stumbling and going the wrong way, while seeking out the right way. Is it any wonder that I have chosen you! As I look to and fro over the earth, I see all of the love in your heart for Me and My heart is melted with mercy and compassion for you. I promise, I will pour down from Heaven, blessings without number, grace without measure and My abiding, unconditional, eternal love. I have chosen you because you have chosen Me and been faithful to Me with a love that has no conditions for, truly, you love Me with an unconditional love.

Forgiven Love, what sin? I don't remember any sin. They have long ago been forgiven and forgotten. The blood of the Lamb, the one perfect, complete and total sacrifice, wiped your slate clean, eternally. Remember, you are cleansed and made holy, once and for all. You do not have to keep coming to Me with every transgression. I AM continually cleansing and healing and restoring. I AM making new and fresh constantly. I AM leading you in the way of holiness. Rest in my promise of new life daily. I AM perfecting all that concerns you and I AM also perfecting you. Be at peace, it is a process. I will not hold back My love until the process is complete. You are loved and cherished right now. Don't carry a heavy load of condemnation. I want you to rejoice in My acceptance of you—in My great and abiding and eternal love for you now, right this very minute. Receive and rejoice in My love.

Beloved, there is, now, no condemnation for those

who are in Christ Jesus. You dwell in Me and I in you—in this union and communion, there is only love. I do not condemn you. All past mistakes and sins have been perpetually washed away—forgiven and forgotten—swept into a sea of forgetfulness.

You are not alone adrift in a stormy sea but My love surrounds you and protects you and guides you. Don't condemn yourself when I don't condemn you or even allow others to condemn you. Learn to love yourself, as I love you, without condemnation—perpetually and eternally forgiven. Rejoice in the freedom of no condemnation, in the joy of a, truly, unconditional love. I will not love you more at some future date, after you have done mighty exploits to show your love for Me. I will not love you more when you have perfected every flaw and corrected every mistake you have ever made or might make. Accept and appreciate My gift of love with no conditions—unconditionally and eternally yours.

I want you to rejoice in My love. Only receive My unconditional love. You don't have to deserve it or earn it or try to keep it from slipping away. There is only joy in receiving. There is no striving or straining. There is no trying to please or measure up to expectations. I love you right where you are—just as you are. I know the reason behind the sin and I forgive you. I know your frailties and your weaknesses. I come not to condemn but to give life abundant—even forevermore. Don't be so afraid of My judgement, which you feel you deserve, that you don't come and receive full pardon and overflowing love and blessing. Trust in My mercy, My lovingkindness and My loving grace raining down upon you as gentle, cleansing, healing, restoring showers of blessing. Receive and rejoice in My love. I love you—unconditionally.

John 3:17–18

For God did not send His Son into the world in order to judge the world guilty, to condemn, to reject, to pass sentence on the world but that the world might find salvation and be saved and made safe and sound through Him.

No one, who has faith in God's Son, will be condemned. The one, who believes in Him, who clings to, trusts in and relies on Him is not judged, for in Him there is no condemnation.

God didn't go to all the trouble of sending His Son merely to point an accusing finger, telling the world how bad it is, He came to help and to put the world right again. Anyone who trusts in Him is acquitted and given eternal life.

Micah 7:18–19

Who is there like You, O God? You forgive iniquity and pass over the transgressions of Your inheritance. You will not stay angry with Your people, for You love to be merciful. You wipe the slate clean of guilt, turning a blind eye and a deaf ear to the past sins of Your purged and precious people. Your compassion is on the way to us. Once more, You will show us Your tender affection, O Lord! You bury our sins in the depths of the sea. You sink them to the bottom of the ocean. You are glad to have pity and lovingkindness. You delight to be gracious. You will take us back in love.

Psalm 103:8–13

Yahweh is tenderness and pity, slow to anger and rich in faithful love. His indignation does not last forever. Adonai is merciful and compassionate. He will not always accuse us, He will not keep His anger forever. The Lord is gracious and rich in grace. He is full of unfailing love.

The Lord has not dealt with us according to the measure of our sins. He never punishes us or treats us as our guilt and iniquities deserve. He will not constantly accuse us.

For as the heavens are high above the earth so great are His mercies and lovingkindness toward those, who reverently and worshipfully fear Him—so vast is His steadfast love to those, who love Him and honor Him. His love is greater than the distance between heaven and earth. As far as the sunrise from the sunset, so far has He separated us from our sins. As far as the east is from the west, so far has He removed our transgressions, our faults, offenses and rebellious acts from us.

As a father loves and pities His children, so the Lord loves and pities those, who fear Him with awe and reverence. The Lord sympathizes with those, who revere Him. For His Own, Yahweh treats them tenderly, with compassion.

Psalm 32:1–2

I find joy in the Lord. I delight in My God. How blessed are those, who have forgiveness of transgressions continually exercised upon them! Blessed are those, whose sin is covered—those, whose wrongs are pardoned.

Blessed, happy, fortunate, to be envied are those, to whom the Lord imputes no iniquity. O the blessedness of the one, whose sin is taken away! Happy, indeed, is the one, to whom the Lord does not ascribe guilt—the one, whom the Eternal has absolved and pardoned—the one, whose sins are wiped away.

How blessed are those, whose rebellion, all of their disobedience and all of their offenses have been blotted out! What relief for the ones that have their record of sin cleared by God. What joy for those, whose lives are lived in complete honesty with nothing false, no deceit and nothing to hide!

How happy you must be! You get a fresh new start. Your slate is wiped clean. God holds nothing against you.

Romans 8:30–39

Having chosen us, He called us to come to Himself and when we came, He declared us not guilty, justified, acquitted and made righteous. He has filled us with Christ's goodness and given us right standing with Himself. He has promised us His glory and His splendor, raising us to a heavenly dignity.

What can we ever say to such wonderful things as these? God is on our side. Who can prevail against us? If God is for us, what does it matter, who may be against us? If God is with us, no one can defeat us.

He, Who did not withhold or spare even His Own Son but gave Him up for us all, will He not also with Him freely and graciously give us all other things as well? With this gift how can He fail to lavish upon us all that He has to give?

Who shall bring any charge against God's elect, the chosen ones of God—when it is God, Himself, Who justifies? Who can accuse the people God has chosen? No one will accuse them because God is the One, Who makes them right. If God says His chosen ones are acceptable to Him, can anyone bring charges against them? No, indeed! Will God? No, for it is God, Who acquits us. Will Christ Jesus, the Messiah, Who died for us and was raised from the dead and now is sitting at the right hand of God, the place of highest honor and is actually pleading our cause as He intercedes for us?

Can anything ever separate us from Christ's love? Shall suffering or anguish, can trouble or problems or affliction and tribulation? Can calamity or distress, hardships or misfortune? Can persecution or imprisonment or homelessness? Can poverty or famine or hunger or lack of food or clothing or destitution? Can threats or hatred or violence or danger or war? Can being in peril for our lives or the sword of our enemies? No, for the Scriptures tell us that for His sake we must be ready to face death at any moment.

In all these things, we are more than conquerors. Gloriously conquering, we win an overwhelming victory through Him, Who has proven His love for us—Christ, Who loved us enough to die for us. The One, Who loves us, always gives us victory in all these difficulties.

He, Who loves us, has enabled us not only to overcome these things but also to emerge triumphant over them.

For I am fully persuaded, I have become absolutely convinced, I have full assurance, I am certain beyond doubt, I am sure of this—that nothing can ever separate us from the love of God. There is nothing in death or life—not in the realm of the spirit or superhuman powers—the angels won't and the demons can't—all of the powers of hell itself cannot keep God's love away. Not in the world as it is or the world as it shall be—not high above the sky or in the deepest ocean or anything else in God's whole universe has any power to come between us and the love of God. Nothing impending and threatening, not our fears for today or our worries about tomorrow, not things present or things to come in the future, not what happens today or what may happen tomorrow, nothing that exists, nothing still to come, not any created thing or anything in all creation, not rulers or principalities, no monarch of the earth or messenger of Heaven, nothing visible or invisible, nothing thinkable or unthinkable can ever come between us and the love of God.

Romans 8:1–2

The conclusion of the matter is this—there is no condemnation at all, no adjudging guilty of wrong, no sentence of condemnation will ever stand against those, who are in union with Christ Jesus—those, who live and walk not after the dictates of the flesh but after the dictates of the Spirit, living lives that are controlled by the Holy Spirit. For the law of the Spirit of Life which is in Christ Jesus, the law of our new being, the new spiritual principle of life from the Life-Giving Spirit has set us free from the law of sin and death.

Psalm 56:9

This one thing I know—God is for me! God is with me and He is on my side! I know I have a God and He is mine!

I know for certain that You are with Me, Lord and I am sure You are on my side!

Chapter 6

Covenant

 HOLY SAINT

Precious Loved One—Yes, you are very precious to Me and you are chosen and loved. You are part of the Bride and yet, you are unique and the only one. You think you chose me but I chose you first and I carefully watched over the events of your life to prepare you for this day. Wait until you see what I have for you—far more than you can possibly conceive! I AM well pleased with My creation of you. You are constantly trying to change and improve upon My beautiful creation of you. I say, See with My eyes and rejoice with Me. Just rest in My creation of you. Don't, continually, try to recreate yourself into your own image of how you think you should be. Rest and rejoice in your uniqueness. Don't strive to meet the expectations of others or fit into the world's mold. Be glad that you don't fit into the world's pattern of what you should be. I have set you apart from the world for My purpose and plan. You are not rejected by the world but I have called you out from it. Your only connection with the world is to show them and tell them that I love them.

Holy Saint of Mine, you are holy, in My eyes, now. You have chosen to turn your back on the world and come apart and lead a set apart life. You have embraced a solitary life, set apart for My service in the Kingdom. You turn to and cleave to your Beloved. You count it all joy to have been chosen for service. I have chosen you and kept you, wholly Mine and holy.

Yes, you are saintly even now. You have been tested and proven and you have proven faithful in every test. So rejoice now in your saintly life that has been tried and tested by fire. You are pure gold in My Kingdom—fit for service now. Today, right now, this very minute you are being used to bless My Beloved. I say, Thank you. I appreciate your eagerness to serve, in love, the love of your life.

2 Thessalonians 1:10

When He comes to be glorified in His saints, on that day, He will be made more glorious in His consecrated people. When Jesus comes to be honored and adored by His holy people, those He has made holy, His coming will mean splendor unimaginable, a breathtaking wonder. All the people, who have believed, will be amazed at Jesus. On that day, when the Lord returns, He will be praised by all, who have faith in Him and belong to Him. He will be marveled at and admired in His glory, reflected in all, who have trusted in, adhered to and relied on Him. He will show how glorious He is, in His saints. He will show how marvelously He has dealt with all the faithful.

And you will be among those praising Him! This includes you. You are in that number. You will be among them because you have accepted the truth, you have trusted and you have believed.

2 Timothy 1:9

It is Jesus, Who delivered us, saved us and called us with a calling, in itself holy and leading to holiness and a life of consecration. He chose us to be His holy people. He summoned us to His side through a call toward holiness. We were divinely summoned with a holy summons.

God called us to a life of holiness as His people. He called us not because of anything of merit that we have done, not because of our good deeds or works. We did nothing to deserve it. His call was because of His Own design and plan, His holy work, in fulfillment of His Own loving purpose. He has shown His love and kindness to us through Christ Jesus. His grace and unmerited favor were given to us in Christ Jesus before the beginning of time.

Colossians 3:12–14

God chose you to be holy. Therefore, Holy and Loved, as the chosen of God, the holy people whom He loves, you are to be clothed in heartfelt compassion. In this new life of love, dress in God's wardrobe with new clothes custom made by your Creator, with His label on them. All old clothes are now obsolete. So, chosen by God for this new life of love, dress in the wardrobe God has picked out for you. Since God chose you to be the holy people whom He loves, you must clothe yourselves in spiritual apparel as His representatives. You are one of those, who are purified and holy and well loved by God, Himself. You are God's people, consecrated and dear to Him—His Beloved.

Put on behavior marked by tenderhearted pity and mercy. Be kind-hearted and gentle. Have a lowly opinion of yourselves. Be humble and have patience, which is tireless. Be long suffering with the power to endure whatever comes with good temper. Be generous to each other. The Lord's generosity to you must be the model of yours. Forgive one another. The Lord has, freely, forgiven you. As He has granted you His forgiveness, you also must be quick to forgive. You must make allowances for each other's faults and forgive the person who offends you.

Therefore, God's Chosen, consecrated to Him and dearly loved by Him, regardless of what else you wear, above all other things, over all the rest—put on love. The most important piece of clothing you wear is love. Never be without it! Love is what holds and binds everything together completely in perfect unity and ideal harmony. Put on divine and self-sacrificial love, which is the binding factor of completeness. Love is the golden chain of all the virtues—the crown of all.

Jeremiah 1:4–5

The Lord spoke His word to me saying, Before I formed you in the womb, I knew all about you. Before you were born, I separated you and set you apart for Myself. I claimed you for My Own. I knew you and approved of you before I formed and fashioned you in the matrix. I chose you as My instrument for My holy purpose and for a special work.

Before your nativity, I hallowed you. Before you were born, I made you holy. Before your birth, I consecrated you. Before you came forth from the womb, I sanctified you. Before you saw the light of day, I had holy plans for you.

1 Peter 1:15–16

As the One, Who called you is holy, you also be holy in all that you do, in all of your conduct, in every aspect of your lives and manner of living. After the model and pattern of the Holy One, Who called you, be holy in every department of your lives, in your entire way of life. For it is written, the Scripture says, You shall be holy, for I AM holy.

John 15:19

You are not of the world, no longer one with it but I have chosen you out of the world. I have picked you out. I have selected you and singled you out from the midst of the world. My choice of you has drawn you out of the world.

1 Thessalonians 3:12–13

May the Lord make you to excel, increase and abound in love one for another and for all people. May the Lord make you grow until you overflow and glow with love. May the Lord give you a rich and even richer love for everyone. May He make your love for all people everywhere wide and full. May the Lord so fill your lives with love that it splashes over on everyone around you. May the Lord establish you in holiness. May your heart be pure and innocent and free from all sin. May the Lord give you inward strength to be holy and without fault or blame. May you stand, imbued with holiness, in the very sight of God.

On the day of His coming, the Lord Jesus will be accompanied by all those, who are holy and consecrated to Him, His Saints, the holy glorified people of God.

1 Thessalonians 5:23

May God, Himself, the very God of Peace, sanctify you through and through and separate you from the profane and make you pure and wholly holy. May God, Himself, the Bringer of Peace, Who gives peace, consecrate you. May He make you perfect in holiness and hallow you completely. Consecrated to God, may your entire being, spirit, soul and body, be preserved and healthy and kept fit and sound at the coming of our Lord Jesus Christ. May you be found free from all blame, without blemish, irreproachable and all together faultless at the appearing of Yeshua, the Messiah. Belonging only to Him, may God, Who makes everything holy and whole, keep you ready for the coming of our Master Jesus Christ.

 FRAGRANCE

Precious Chosen One—I will give life, to your life! I came that you might have life and have it more abundantly— life to the full and spilling over with an abundance of joy and rejoicing, peace and love and a bountiful supply of blessings.

I will so permeate your life and your very being that you will leave My sweet fragrance wherever you go. It will linger after you have gone. Others will continue to breathe in the sweet aroma of My Presence and want more and want to keep it with them always. That aroma, alone, will turn their hearts to seeking after it and finding Me. You don't have to say anything or do anything, just take and impart that sweet fragrance and they will follow after it and find Me.

Beloved, you are a very special treasure in My Kingdom. You are treasured by Me, by your family and friends and you are a surprise and a delightful treasure to strangers. Your loving openness and vulnerability are a refreshing and a very special gift of My love to those around you. My anointing oil has a sweet, lingering and lasting fragrance that blesses and exudes new life. Watch those around you breath in deeply and relax and be at peace. Watch new life begin to take root and grow into a holy, eternal life. I will allow you to see with spiritual eyes and see the seeds, you have scattered over the earth, sprout and grow into a mighty harvest. You will begin to see, with amazement, the fruit coming forth from all of the seeds you have lovingly and joyfully scattered over the earth. Continue doing just what you have been doing! You have blessed My Kingdom more than you know. Not only do you receive blessing but you bless. I AM blessed and touched by your heart of love. Those around you are touched and blessed. They are healed, restored and refreshed with a new life of love, a promise of hope and a fresh new start. They have stumbled upon great treasure and priceless gifts that they will take away and share with others.

Thank you, for being a precious treasure in My Kingdom. Thank you, for imparting My sweet life-giving fragrance wherever you go.

Your life turned to Me and following after Me, is a sweet savor and a sweet smelling sacrifice unto Me. Your prayers are a sweet smelling incense offered upon the alter of sacrifice in loving concern for others. I promise, I have heard and recorded every one—not one has been lost or gone unheeded. If they have not been answered yet, it is because they are in process and being now completed. You can rest in answered prayer. The answer is always Yes and never No.

I have placed the desire in your heart and I will delight to give you the desire of your heart. I delight in delighting you—My Bride, the delight of My heart.

2 Corinthians 2:14–16

Thanks be to God, Who in Christ always, constantly and unfailingly leads us in a triumphal procession as trophies of Christ's victory! Through us, He spreads and makes evident everywhere, the fragrance of what it means to know Him. He employs us to diffuse that fragrance everywhere—a breath bringing life. Wherever we go, the Lord uses us to spread the Good News like a sweet perfume. Through us, He is making manifest all over the world, the experiential knowledge of Himself. Wherever we go God uses us to make clear what it means to know Christ. It is like an aroma from life to life, a vital fragrance, living and fresh, which fills the air.

To God, there is a sweet, wholesome fragrance in our lives. It is the fragrance of Christ within us. We are, indeed, the incense offered by Christ to God, the fragrance of Christ, ascending to God and the sweet savor of Christ made manifest to those around us, who are achieving salvation or on the road to ruin. To one, a warning of death and doom, a deadly fume, a poisonous stench, a fatal odor—to the other, the sweet perfume of life that leads to more and better life, the refreshing vital fragrance of life that brings life.

Wherever I go, thank God, He makes My life a constant pageant of triumph in Christ, a perpetual victory parade. I live for God—a fragrance of Christ. He uses Me to display and spread and diffuse the sweet perfume that results from knowing Him. Yes, I am the fragrance of Christ, the sweet aroma of life, which leads to life.

Thanks be to God, Who has made us in the pattern of Christ!

Ephesians 5:1–2

Do as God does. Take Him as your pattern. Be imitators of God. Copy Him and follow His example in everything. As well-beloved children imitate their father, watch what God does then do it. Mostly, what God does is love you. You are His and He loves you. Keep company with Him and learn a life of love. Observe how Christ loved us and gave everything of Himself for us. Love like that. Let love rule your lives. Order your behavior in the way of love. Walk in love, esteeming and delighting in one another. Christ gave Himself up for us, an offering and a sacrifice that was a sweet fragrance, a sweet smelling savor that was sweetness itself. God is well pleased with Christ's love for you. Christ's love is like a sweet perfume to God, a fragrant and acceptable sacrifice. Follow the example of Jesus—practice living in love. Live a life of love.

 SEEDS

See, Beloved, how I have promised to minister to you night and day. Even while you are resting in Me, I will be with you accomplishing My purpose and plan. Thank you, for being a willing vessel and a ready receiver. I have prepared you for such a time as this. As you go, to and fro, over the earth, you will leave precious seeds of faith and hope and love. I will see that the seeds fall on fertile ground and quickly multiply into the Kingdom. They will mature and produce seeds, which will produce seeds. I will bring a rich harvest and a bounteous crop of blessing in the land. I will lovingly tend and watch over each tiny seed.

The seeds of earth that are full of life and fertile— seeds that sprout and grow into abundant life and fruit, to feed and bless the earth, amaze you but the seeds planted into My kingdom are so far above earthly seeds. The seeds planted into the Kingdom go on multiplying for all eternity and abound and multiply into eternal life in all directions and areas. There is life in the Word and there is life in the fruit of the Spirit, which multiplies by contact, by example, by thought and by deed.

Wherever you go, you leave behind beautiful, fertile, life-filled and life-giving seeds that quickly multiply into the Kingdom. Your very presence filled with the Fruit of the Spirit produces an abundant crop of blessing unto eternal life. Love, peace, joy, faith, patience, meekness and self-control abide but the greatest is love. Love produces love for all eternity.

You have given and planted seeds of love and those seeds are ripening into an abundant harvest. Seeds of love, planted in the Kingdom, reap an amazing yield and return. They multiply in all directions. Watch the wind of My Holy Spirit carry the seeds far and wide. See how they fall and take root, sprout and grow into maturity and produce abundant, beautiful fruit that produces more fruit. The seeds of love that you have scattered so joyfully over the earth are as bread cast on the water that will return after many days. Get ready to rejoice in the harvest. The return will fill you with such joy! You will be humbled by the love and receive the yield with gratitude. You will be thankful for the ways of the Kingdom on earth. The fruitful seeds of the Kingdom will endure forever. They go on bearing fruit throughout eternity.

You have scattered seeds of love with no thought of return and you have planted for the joy of blessing but you will be surprised and thrilled by the return, to you.

Get ready to receive and rejoice! Rejoice in the return, the abundant, amazing yield of seeds planted in the Kingdom. Favor upon favor, gift upon gift, blessing upon blessing and love upon love is on the way!

Galatians 5:22–23

When we live God's way, He brings gifts into our lives—the beautiful fruit of affection for others, a compassionate heart and exuberance about life. God's Spirit makes us loving and happy, peaceful and faithful, good and kind, patient and self-controlled. The work which His Presence within accomplishes is joy and gladness, the strength of gentleness, meekness and humility, modesty and chastity, benevolence and generosity, temperance, tolerance and an even temper, forbearance, long-suffering, trustfulness and graciousness.

There is no law against behaving in any of these ways—no law against those, who practice such things. No one says these things are wrong. No law forbids them.

Luke 8:15

A sower went out to sow his seeds. Seeds sown in right soil represent the good ground of honest and true, good-hearted people. When they hear the Word, God's Message, they embrace it, cling to it and hold fast to it. They keep it and retain it in a pure and noble, virtuous and worthy, receptive heart. They steadily, with patience, bring forth fruit and produce a huge harvest. In their constancy, they go on faithfully producing good things. They endure and go on steadfastly, perseveringly producing a good crop and yielding a great harvest. They take God's teachings to heart and bear fruit through thick and thin. They produce good fruit, despite what life may bring.

Proverbs 11:18

He, who sows seeds of lovingkindness and righteousness in every area and relation, shall have a sure reward, permanent and satisfying. A generous man is his own benefactor and is recompensed in his own soul. A kindly man does himself good. The reward of the godly will last.

Isaiah 32:20

God will bless you. Happy and fortunate are you, who cast your seed upon the water when the river overflows its banks, for the seed will sink into the mud. When the water subsides, the plant will spring up. You will find it after many days and reap an abundant harvest.

God will greatly bless His people. Wherever they plant seed, bountiful crops will spring up.

Mark 4:31–32

The Kingdom of God is like a grain of mustard seed which, when sown to the ground, is the smallest of all seeds upon the earth. Yet, after it is sown, it grows up and becomes the greatest of all garden herbs and puts out branches so large that the birds of the air are able to make nests and dwell in its shade.

James 3:18

A harvest that has God's approval comes from the seeds of peace planted by peacemakers.

Psalm 126:6

Those, who sow in tears, shall reap in joy and singing. Those, who go forth bearing precious seeds, weeping at needing their supply of grain for sowing, shall doubtless come again with rejoicing, bringing their sheaves with them.

You may go weeping, carrying your bag of precious seeds for sowing but you will come home with songs and shouts of joy carrying your harvest of bundles of grain.

Bring rain to our drought-stricken lives, Lord—so that those, who plant with heavy hearts in despair, will come home at harvest, laughing with armloads of blessings.

Mark 4:26–29

The Kingdom of God is like a man who scatters seed into the ground. Night and day, while he sleeps and when he is awake, the seed is sprouting and growing. The seed springs up, although he has no idea how it happens. Without any help from anyone, the earth acting by itself, produces first the blade, then the stalk, then the ear, then the full grain in the ear. When the grain is ripe, immediately he sends forth the reapers and puts in the sickle because the harvest stands ready. Harvest time has come!

Psalm 97:11–12

A harvest of light is sown by the Righteous One. Light is scattered abroad by the Righteous One. Light is sown for the uncompromisingly righteous and strewn along their pathway. Joy is sown for the upright in heart—the irrepressible joy that comes from consciousness of God's favor and protection. Light seeds are planted in the souls of God's people. Joy seeds are planted in good heart soil. Radiance is sown for the virtuous and the just and gladness is sown for the good.

Light dawns for you. Light will show you the way and fill you with happiness. Be glad in the Lord. Find joy in Him and praise His unforgettable holiness. Rejoice because of what the Lord has done. Give thanks as you remember how holy He is. Be thankful for your consciousness of His holiness. Give thanks as you recall His sacred name. Acclaim His holy name! May all, who are godly, rejoice and be happy in the Lord. May they praise His holy name!

Ephesians 5:9–10

The Fruit of the Spirit consists of every form of kindly goodness, uprightness of heart and right living. The effect of the Light of the Spirit is every kind of beneficence. This Light within you produces everything that is wholesome. This Light brings a rich harvest of what is good, right and true. Goodness, justice and truth spring up with this Light, verifying what pleases the Lord.

Try to learn in your experience what is, fully, pleasing to the Lord. Submit everything to, the test of, the approval of the Lord. Let your lives be constant living proofs of what is acceptable to Him.

 SOLDIER

Beloved Christian Soldier—First and foremost, this letter is written to your heart that is so ready to receive A Long Love Letter *from Me. Thank you, for being a ready receiver and a receptacle for My love. Thank you, for taking in and giving out. Thank you, for caring for others and for sharing My love with them. Thank you, for telling of My love and showing My love to others. To be on the front lines of My Army, you must mow them down with love. The greatest lovers become the highest ranked Generals among Christian Soldiers.*

Does Mother Teresa look like one you would send

to the front lines of the Army? She was right there on the front lines, in the heat of the battle. She was tough and unrelenting and determined to love no matter the cost. She spent all she had, loving and being an example of love. She loved not her life unto the death and she over came the enemy with the word of her testimony.

My Soldiers not only plunder Satan's kingdom, they rob him of his power and his victims in hand-to-hand combat and commando tactics. They shoot to kill, with kindness, to release the captives and loose those held in bondage. My front line Army is fearless, as they love not their lives unto the death, always loving those around them and leading them to the light, regardless of the cost. Some of them have given up all—houses, family, possessions, even all of their own hopes and dreams and plans, to answer the call. They take up arms and march to the front lines, armed with a weapon that is undefeatable. It is both ageless and eternal. It is state of the art, the latest and most powerful tool to take out enemy forces, a weapon that will bring them to their knees in surrender. They are winning the battle with love—My secret weapon of pure, unadulterated love. No enemy can stand against this weapon, used with expert care by My Defense Force. Watch them overcome enemy forces and set the captives free—who will join the Army and turn and free other captives.

Remember, it has been said of you that you are God's Commando. You drop a Bible and run and the damage has been done—the truth has been revealed. The captives are set free and those dwelling in darkness have seen a great light. You don't even realize that you have been a part of the Great End-Time Army, marching as to war, to bring in the Last Great Harvest. You have been delighted to have been chosen—drafted into service. You have been thrilled to have been used regardless of your age and limitations and weakness. You have so willingly laid down your life that others might live. You don't even know how much I have used you, right on the very front lines of My Army. You have been a General without even knowing it. In humble service, you have served with great love because of your great love for Me and I say, Well done good and faithful Soldier!

The very best is yet to come. You are well-trained and well-prepared to move up in the Service. You have been faithful over a little—I now promote you to being in charge of much. Rejoice in your promotion, in your rank and file. Your yielded spirit and your obedience in quickly following commands has allowed Me freedom to live and move and have My Being in and through you. Thank you, beautiful Bride of Mine, great and mighty and fearless lover and worshiper. I have received your gift and I honor you, in My Kingdom, with My Name and everything that I own as a loving bridegroom shares all that he has with his beloved, cherished bride.

Revelation 12:11

They overcame the accuser, the one, who has been accusing them before our God, day and night, by means of the Blood of the Lamb and by the word of their testimony. They defeated and conquered the accuser by virtue of the Lamb's spilled blood and by the preaching of the Word, the Message to which they bore testimony. Love for life did not deter them. Even when faced with death, they did not spare themselves. They were willing to die a martyr's death. They did not consider their lives too dear or too precious to lay them down. They did not love their lives so much that they refused to give them up. They did not shrink back or hold on to or cling to life but they triumphed by the truth which they proclaimed. The fearless declaration of their faith has won for them an eternal victory.

1 Corinthians 13

If I can speak in the tongues of men and even angels—if I speak in every human and angelic language but have not love and charity for others, I will be making a meaningless noise. If I have not that love inspired by God's love for us and in us, God's love produced in the heart by the Holy Spirit, I would be only a loud clanging bell or a noisy cymbal. I would be no better than a resounding, echoing gong.

If I have the gift of inspired preaching—if I have prophetic powers to interpret the divine will and purpose—if I fathom all of the sacred truths—if I am wise and possess all knowledge—if there is no secret hidden from me, no knowledge too deep for me—if I know everything about everything and even if I have perfect and sufficient faith so complete that I can remove mountains but have not love, God's love in me, I am nothing, a useless nobody. There is no value to my life.

If I dole out all that I have to the poor and bestow my goods to feed the hungry—if I distribute all I possess in charity but have not love, it is no good to me.

Even if I welcome a martyr's death—if I surrender and sacrifice my body to be burned at the stake—if I am burned alive for preaching the Gospel but have not love, I'm not in the least benefited. I gain nothing. It profits me nothing at all if I am without love.

Love is gentle, benign and pervading, penetrating the whole nature, mellowing out all that would have been harsh and austere.

Love suffers and endures long. Love is very patient and very kind. Love meekly and patiently bears ill treatment from others. The love, of which I speak, is slow to lose patience. It looks for a way of being constructive.

Love impels one to deny self, for the sake of the loved one. Love is gracious. Love is never envious. It never boils over with jealousy.

Love does not sing its own praises. Love is not arrogant or conceited. It does not put on airs neither does it cherish ideas of its own importance. Love is not inflated with ego and pride. Love is not pompous or boastful. It is not vainglorious or puffed up. It is never anxious to impress and does not display itself haughtily.

Love does not act unbecomingly or behave unseemly. It is never indecent and never deals perversely.

Love is not rude or unmannerly, demanding its own way. Love is not selfish or self-seeking. Love cares more for others than itself. God's love in us does not insist on its rights. Love never seeks its own advantage.

Love is not touchy or irritable or fretful. Love is not resentful. Love does not brood over injuries. Love is not easily provoked or aroused to anger. Love does not lose its temper or fly off the handle. Love never nurses its wrath to keep it warm. Love bears no malice.

Love can stand any kind of treatment. Love does not take offense or store up grievances. Love pays no attention to a suffered wrong.

It keeps no record of wrongs. It takes no account of evil done to it. It thinks no evil.

Love does not rejoice at injustice, unrighteousness or iniquity but rejoices when right and truth prevail. Love takes no pleasure in wrong doing and is never glad when others go wrong. Love does not revel when others grovel but delights in the victory of truth.

Love always protects, always perseveres. Love bears all things— believes all things. Love bears up under anything and everything that comes. Love is ever ready and always eager to believe the very best in others. Love's first instinct is to believe in people. Love is always ready to make allowances. Love overlooks faults. There is nothing love cannot face.

Love is always supportive and loyal and trusting. Love is always hopeful under all circumstances, at all times. Love never regards anyone or anything as hopeless.

Love never loses faith. There is no limit to its faith. Love never gives up.

Love gives us the power to endure everything without weakening. Nothing can happen that can break love's spirit. It does not lose heart or courage. Love endures all things and remains strong.

Faith, hope and love abide. These are the three greats that will keep on and last forever.

Faith is the conviction and belief, respecting man's relation to God and divine things.

Hope is the joyful, confident expectation of eternal salvation.

Love is the true affection for God and others, growing out of God's love for us and in us.

Have faith, steadfastly, in God. Hope unswervingly. Love extravagantly. The very best—the greatest of these is love.

Love never fails or falls away. Love can out last anything. Love never comes to an end. Love lasts forever. Love is eternal.

Earnestly seek to acquire this love. Make it your aim and your greatest quest. Let love then be your highest goal. Follow after the way of love—let love be your guide. Desire it with your whole heart. Put love first. You must want love more than anything else. Spare no effort to obtain and keep love.

Be, constantly, pursuing this love—earnestly, endeavoring to possess it. Go after love as if your life depended on it—because it does!

 COMMAND

Beloved Bride—As I send you out into the world to deliver both of My love letters, I send you with only one commandment—for in carrying out the one, you have kept the perfect law, perfectly. I have made it very easy and simple for you to keep, ever before you, one commandment. My command is—love.

Let My love so permeate your very being that when you open your mouth, out will pour forth a flood of love. Be so filled with My love that when you look on others, it will melt their hearts with My love. Carry My heart out into the world and heal the brokenhearted. With great compassion and love, lift up and help the wounded, the hurt, the injured and the dying.

I send you forth, filled to the brim and spilling over with My love. It will spill over and splash over on anyone, who comes near. It will rain down and soak any, who will stop and listen. It will bless and comfort. It will bring hope, new trust and new faith in all of My promises. I promise you—My love.

John 13:34–35

I give you a new commandment that you should love one another. Just as I have loved you, so you too should love one another. You must love. Prove to the world that you are Mine. They will know you by your love.

By this shall all people know that you are My disciples, if you love one another.

1 Peter 1:22

Now you can have sincere love for each other as brothers and sisters because you were cleansed from your sins when you accepted the truth of the Good News. You have purified your hearts for sincere affection.

See that you love one another with a warm love that comes from a pure heart.

Love one another whole-heartedly with all your strength.

Love one another cordially and consistently.

Love one another earnestly and deeply with all your heart.

Love one another intensely and fervently.

Love one another as if your lives depended on it.

You must keep on loving one another!

1 John 4:20–21

Beloved, we must love one another. If we love one another, God abides in us. He loves and remains in us and His love is brought to completion, to full maturity and perfected in us. God does, actually, live in us and His love is, truly, in our hearts. If we say that we love God and don't love each other, the truth is not in us—for those, who don't love others, whom they have seen cannot love God, Whom they have not seen.

We know and understand, by observation and by experience,

the love God cherishes for us. God is love. Those, who continue in love, dwell in God and God dwells in them. In this union and communion with Him, our love is made perfect.

The command God has given to us is—love God and one another.

1 Peter 4:8

Above all things have intense and unfailing love, for one another, for love hides a multitude of sins. Be keen to love for love cancels innumerable sins. Love draws a veil over many a sin. Love throws a cover over countless sins. Love forgives and disregards the offenses of others. Love makes up for practically anything and overcomes nearly everything. Love one another earnestly and warmly. Be fervent in your love. Keep your love at full strength. Keep on loving, actively and constantly. Before all other things, show deep love for each other. Most of all, love one another as if you life depended on it.

Romans 13:8–10

Pay your debts as they come due but never finish paying the debt of love for others. Owe no debt except the debt that binds us to love everyone. Keep the standing, perpetual debt of love. Always owe love. Let love be your only debt.

The one, who loves others has fulfilled and obeyed the whole law and satisfied all that the law demands, meeting all of its requirements.

In the law, there are many commands such as: be faithful in marriage, do not murder, do not steal and do not want what belongs to others but all of the Law is summed up in the one command—love others as much as you love yourself. No one who loves others will hurt or harm them. Love does no wrong to one's neighbors. Love is all that the law demands. Loving is obeying all—the one golden rule. When you add up everything in the law, the sum total is love.

1 Peter 3:8

And now this word to all of you—all of you should be of one and the same mind, united in the spirit, in agreement and feeling, one for another. Like one big happy family, be full of sympathy toward each other, loving one another with tender hearts in a spirit of humility. Be compassionate and courteous. You must be deeply concerned for others. Never exchange verbal abuse for verbal abuse or insult for insult. You must never repay injury for injury. On the contrary, you must ask God to bless those, who treat you badly. Be constantly blessing, for this very purpose you were called. Your vocation is to bless and to inherit a blessing. Be a blessing and be blessed!

Matthew 28:19–20

Go then and make people, of every nation, into disciples and followers of Mine. Baptize them, immersing them into the reality of the Father, the Son and the Holy Spirit. Teach them to keep all of the commandments and every rule and to observe everything I have commanded you.

Remember, I AM with you always, on every occasion and all days, perpetually and uniformly, to the very close of the age, to the end of the world. There is not a day when I will not be with you to the end of time.

2 Corinthians 13:11

The God of Love, the Source of love, affection, goodwill and benevolence toward others and the Author and Promoter of peace be with you. Live in peace and God, the Bringer of peace and love, will be on your side.

John 13:13, 17

You call Me Rabbi, your Teacher, your Master, your Lord and you are right, for so I AM. If I then your Teacher and Lord, have washed your feet, you must be ready to wash one another's feet. I have given you this example so that you should do, in turn, what I have done for you. Treat others as I have treated you.

I say unto you, the servant is not superior to his Master and Lord. No apostle, no emissary, no messenger is greater than he, who sent him. You will be blessed when you follow My example. Happy are you, if you act accordingly. A blessing will rest upon you, if you will act on what you know. This is the path of blessing.

 GOD'S PEACE

Beloved Bride—First and foremost, charity begins at home. This is a great truth to be taken to heart. You can only give from your overflow so come and be filled to overflowing with My love and My peace. What I ask is not a hard thing. I will fill you as you rest in Me. Receive My peace and My love in such a vast, overflowing supply that it will spill over and splash over on everyone who comes near. In a day of trouble, your overflowing peace will calm the storm and still the frightened hearts around you. In a day of hate, your love will spill over and produce an epidemic of love, contagious and rapidly spreading. Rest and receive My peace. Rejoice and bask in My love. I AM here and there is nothing to fear.

Don't forget Beloved, I have promised a peace that passes all understanding—a constant, undisturbed, quiet and peaceful, portion of peace. In a world that longs for peace you have an abundant supply. I will envelope you with a warm blanket of peace, a protective barrier against all harm, a safe and comforting cocoon of peace surrounding you at all times. To be concerned, to be anxious or worried is not part of My plan for you. Complete and total trust and faith in Me is a very necessary part of the perfect peace I have planned for you. Perfect, undisturbed, constant peace is a precious and priceless gift of My love.

You can lie down in complete peace and rest in undisturbed peace. You can rise up and live and work and stay in a peace, the world can't even understand.

I bless you with peace. It is a gift to be guarded and cherished. It is a blessing beyond compare. I anoint you as My Messenger of Peace. I send you forth as My Ambassador and My Emissary of Perfect Peace. Even in a time of war and turmoil and unrest, you will rest in peace. In this world—at this time—in these conditions—I promise you peace. It is yours now and forever because I love you.

John 14:27

Peace is My parting gift to you. Peace I bequeath to you. Peace I leave with you. My Own peace, I now give to you. I AM leaving you with a gift of peace of mind and heart. I give you peace—the kind of peace that only I can give, a peace the world cannot give or understand. My peace is nothing like the fragile peace the world gives. I now give you My perfect peace.

Do not let your heart be troubled neither let it be afraid. Don't let your heart be dismayed or distressed or disquieted. Stop allowing yourselves to be agitated, upset and disturbed. Do not permit yourselves to be fearful, intimidated, cowardly or unsettled. Don't let your heart lose its courage.

Peace is My farewell to you. My last gift to you is peace.

John 16:33

I have told you these things so that in Me you may have perfect peace. In your union with Me, you will find and keep undisturbed, abiding, constant peace. In Me, you will have all that makes for true happiness.

In the world, you have trials and tribulations, distress and frustration, affliction and suffering but trusting in Me, you will be unshakable, assured and deeply at peace. In this world, you will experience difficulties and trouble but take heart. Never lose heart! I have won the victory for you. I have been victorious over the world with a permanent victory.

Be of good cheer. Be brave and courageous. I have overcome the world. I have deprived it of its power to harm you. I have conquered it for you.

1 Thessalonians 3:16

May the Lord of Peace, Himself, give you peace always, in all ways. May the Giver of Peace, Jehovah Shalom, bestow His peace upon you. May He grant you His peace, continually, at all times, under all circumstances, in every possible condition, no matter what happens.

May the Lord, from Whom all peace comes, be with you and bless you. May He give you every blessing at all times, in every way.

Philippians 4:7

God's peace shall be yours—that tranquil state of a soul assured of its salvation through Christ and so fearing nothing from God and being content with its earthly lot, of whatever sort that is, shall garrison and mount guard over your hearts and minds in Christ Jesus. God's peace will stand guard over your thoughts and emotions because your life is linked forever with the life of Christ Jesus.

God's peace will keep you safe and protect you. God will bless you with peace. His peace will keep your thoughts and your hearts quiet and at rest as you trust in Christ. His peace will control the way you think and feel.

You will experience God's peace, which is far greater and more wonderful than the human mind can understand. God's peace transcends and surpasses all our powers of thought and is beyond all our dreams. It goes beyond anything we can imagine. God's peace surpasses all comprehension and is deeper than all knowledge.

 BRIDE

Beloved Bride—I have chosen you from among the many because of My great and abiding love for you. Long ago I chose you, even from the foundation of the earth, to be My wedded wife—My heart's desire. I rejoice that your answer has always been, with all your heart and soul, your very being, you have replied, "Yes, I will! With all of the love that is in me or ever possible for me, I will! I will follow after You with all of my heart. I will serve you with deepest devotion. I will take Your name and become a totally new creation in the eyes of the world. I will joyfully come to live with You in Your house forever!"

I have seen your heart from the very beginning and My heart has melted with your simple childlike faith and trust and with your beautiful attentive ears longing to hear from your Beloved. You are ever listening for My whispers of love and looking for My tender, loving care and concern. You have chosen silence over all the sounds of earth, so that your ears will not miss a single word from your Beloved. Thank you, for listening and being attuned to My voice.

My Own, you have beautiful hands and feet. How beautiful are the feet of those who bring good news, delivering hope and blessing and new life in the earth. You will dance for pure joy on the path I have chosen for you. Thank you, for being My hands and My feet in the earth. Your lovely hands of service have always been open and generous in giving out what you have received. In lifting up the fallen, those, who have stumbled along the way, you have been My hands reaching out, in love, in the earth.

Beloved, I see your beautiful spiritual eyes and My heart is glad. Thank you, for looking longer and deeper and higher and wider with eyes of love. Thank you, for searching beyond what you see with your physical eyes to find My purpose and plan. Thank you, for your lovely eyes of faith.

Dear Heart, you have a beautiful heart. The world looks on the outward appearance but I look on the heart and My heart rejoices at your heart. I have seen your heart filled to the brim and spilling over with love and compassion for those around you. I see a heart broken for others. I see a heart that longs to reach out and help and lift up and share the Good News. I have heard your heart's cry—"Lord, they need Bibles! Help me, Lord, to put a Bible in their hand. It will help them, Lord. It will give them life and hope and joy. Please, Lord, let's feed the starving souls with the Bread of Life, Your holy Word, the Bible."

I have seen the tears of your heart for the lost and dying and your longing to share the Gospel, the great Good News. You are so, thoroughly, convinced that it will bring life to the dead and dying. You have touched My heart with your beautiful heart.

Is it any wonder that I have chosen you to carry My Word and My love letter and to personally deliver them to My beloved Bride? I will go with you. Together we will take new life and fresh hope and our hearts filled to the brim and spilling over with love for the wounded and the hurt. We will save them from their plight—with our love.

Beloved, truly, you will be carrying and dispersing in the earth a double portion of love. My Word is a pouring forth of all of the love in My heart. Their hearts will be touched and their broken hearts will be mended by all of the love in My heart.

As you scatter fertile seeds of love and faith and hope and joy, I will see that the precious seeds fall on fertile ground and reap a mighty harvest. I have prepared the soil to receive the life-filled, life-giving seed. I will care for each tiny seed that will grow and mature and ripen and produce more seeds.

You have been faithful with a little. You are prepared and you are now ready to be sent into the Kingdom bearing precious life-giving seeds. I will go with you and convince them of My unconditional, undying, everlasting, eternal, unending love.

1 Samuel 16:7

People look at the outside of a person—God looks at the inside. They look at the outward visible appearance but God looks and sees a person's thought and intentions. People look at the face and judge others by what they look like—the Lord looks into the heart and judges what is inside of the heart.

Ephesians 1:17–19

I pray that the God of glory, the Source of everything glorious, the All-Glorious Father, to Whom all glory belongs, may grant you a spirit of wisdom and revelation. May He give you true insight into mysteries and secrets. May the eyes of your heart be flooded with light so that you can know and understand the hope to which He has called you and how rich is His glorious inheritance in the saints, His set-apart ones. May the eyes of your understanding be enlightened to see the magnificence and the splendor of the inheritance promised to Christians. Then you will discover the blessings that will be yours and the wonderful future He has promised to those He has called.

May you receive that inner illumination of the Spirit to be able to know our Lord Christ Jesus better. May you be able to know Him with a growing and personal knowledge, a deep and intimate comprehension of Him.

May your eyes be focused and clear so that you can see exactly what He is calling you to do. May you grasp the immensity of the glorious way of life He has for Christians and how vast the resources of His power available to those, who believe—the transcendent greatness of His power in us believers. My prayer is that your mind may be opened to see and enlightened to understand the immeasurable, unlimited, surpassing greatness of His power in and for us, who believe. Endless energy and boundless strength!

I pray that your inward eyes may be illumined to understand what it means to know God. May He enlighten your innermost vision to see the riches of His glory. Then you will have the confidence that He calls you to have and you will understand the glorious wealth that God's people inherit.

Matthew 13:16–17

Blessed are your eyes for they see! How fortunate you are to have eyes that see! Privileged and to be envied are your eyes because they do see and your ears because they do hear. Truly, I tell you, many prophets and those, who were upright and in right standing with God, yearned and longed to see what you now see and did not see it and to hear what you now hear and did not hear it. I assure you that many of God's people would have given anything to see what you are seeing and to hear what you are hearing but they never had the chance.

Isaiah 50:4–5

The Sovereign Lord has taught me what to say. He has given me His words of wisdom so that I know what to say to all of the weary ones. The Lord God has given me the tongue of a disciple that I should know how to speak a word in season. He has given me a timely word and the skill to console with a word of comfort. The Lord has given me understanding. He has opened my understanding to His will. The Eternal has given me the tongue of the learned that I may rightly answer the ungodly. Elohim has given me the ability to speak as one well taught. My Lord, Yahweh has given me the tongue of the instructed that I should know how to sustain and succor the fainting with discourse. Adonai gives me the ability to teach so that I will know what to say to make the weak strong. The Almighty Lord will teach me what to say to encourage and lift up tired people with a word.

The Lord wakes me, morning by morning, to hear as a disciple—as one, who is taught. The Lord wakes my ear to hear. He has made me willing to listen. I will listen like a student. He makes me eager to hear what He is going to teach me. He alerts my ear to learn my lessons taught by Him. The Lord helps me to learn. He wakes me up and opens my ears to listen as one ready to take orders. The Lord has spoken to me. I will not go back to sleep or pull the covers over my head—I will follow His orders. I will not turn away. I will not turn against Him or stop following Him. I will not be rebellious or resist him. I will obey!

Isaiah 52:7

How beautiful upon the mountains are the feet of those, who bring Good News! It is a beautiful sight to see even the feet of someone coming to preach peace. How welcome is the coming of those, who preach the Good News of His good things! They hasten over the hills to preach the Gospel of salvation and proclaim prosperity. How beautiful is the person, who comes proclaiming victory, good fortune and happiness! The herald hastens over the hills with the great glad tidings, Your God is King and He reigns! How lovely are the feet of those, who publish the Good News of God's goodness, the Gospel of relief and deliverance.

What a beautiful sight, a messenger announcing the Good News, You are saved! There will be peace. All is well. A sight to take your breath away! Grand processionals of people all telling of all of the good things of God!

Proverbs 31:20

She opens her hand to the poor. Yes, she reaches out her filled hands to the needy whether in body, mind or spirit. She extends a helping hand to the wretched and the oppressed. She holds out her hands and lends a hand to the forlorn. She is open-handed and generous. She gives generously. Her purse is ever open to those in need. She is quick to assist. She reaches out to embrace anyone in need.

Matthew 25:34–36, 40

Then the King will say, Come, you have My Father's blessing resting upon you. You have earned His blessing. You are favored of God and appointed to salvation. Come and receive as your own, the Kingdom prepared for you from the foundation of the universe. Take possession of the Kingdom reserved and destined for you from the creation of the world. Come into your inheritance. For I was hungry and you gave Me food. I was thirsty and you gave Me drink. I was a homeless stranger and you made Me your guest. I was alone and away from home and you received Me in your home. You welcomed Me and lodged Me and entertained Me. I was poorly clad and you provided cloths for Me. When I was sick, you came to My help and comforted Me. You took care of Me with ministering care. When I was in prison you came to see Me. You visited Me with hope.

The King will say, I can guarantee you this truth, whatever you did for one of My brothers or sisters, no matter how unimportant they seemed, you did it for Me. You have my solemn assurance that when you rendered such services to one of the humblest— that was Me. You were doing it unto Me.

Ephesians 5:25–27

Christ loved the church and gave Himself up for her. He gave His life with a love marked by giving, not getting. He sacrificed Himself for the church with a self-sacrificial love that

He might purify and sanctify her.

In order to have the church as His very Own, standing before Him in all her glory, He cleansed her by the washing of the Word. He washed her by baptism and the indwelling Word of God that she might be holy and faultless, without spot or wrinkle or any imperfection. Christ's love makes the church whole, like the bride in all her beauty, immaculate in stainless glory and radiant with holiness.

Revelation 19:7–9

Let us rejoice and be glad! Let us shout for joy, exulting and triumphant! Let us celebrate and ascribe to Him glory and honor for the wedding day and the marriage of the Lamb at last has come and His Bride has made herself ready.

She is given a bridal gown of bright and shining, radiant and dazzling, resplendent linen. The finest of clean and white linen represents godly living and conduct, right standing with God and virtuous good deeds done by God's saints, God's holy people.

The Angel said to me, Write this down. Blessed, happy, to be envied are those, who are called to the Marriage Supper of the Lamb—those, who have been invited to the Feast. He said to me further, these are the true words, the genuine and exact declaration, and the very words of God.

Song of Songs 2:4

He has brought me to the banqueting house and His banner over me is love. Love waves a protecting and comforting banner over my head when I am near Him. He brings me to the banqueting hall and looks at me with love. His eyes feast on me and everyone can see how much He loves me.

Isaiah 62:4–5

You will no longer be spoken of as forsaken. No more will you be thought of as abandoned, rejected, desolate or God-forsaken. You will be called Beulah, happily married and My wedded wife, for the Lord claims you as His Own. You will be called Hephzibah, My delight is in her, for Yahweh has found delight in you. The Lord is delighted and pleased with you. Jehovah has tender affection for you. Your new name will be The Bride because the Lord loves you.

As a bridegroom thrills to his bride so shall your God thrill to you. As a young man cares for his bride, your God will protect and care for you with joy. As a bridegroom rejoices over his bride, the Lord will rejoice over you.

Hosea 2:19–20

I will betroth you to Myself forever. Yes, I will loyally betroth you with unfailing devotion and steadfast love, in a bond of goodness and lovingkindness and in compassion and mercy. I will bond you to Me forever in chains of righteousness and justice. I will take you to be My wife in stability and fidelity, in faithful love and tenderness. I will love you with all of My heart. You will know Me then as you never have before. You will recognize, become acquainted with, give heed to, appreciate and cherish the Lord. You will learn of and understand the Eternal God. I will be true to you, My Wife.

Ephesians 3:14–19

When I think of the wisdom and the scope of God's plan, I fall to my knees and pray to the Father, the Creator of everything in Heaven and on earth. Seeing the greatness of His plan, I pray that from His glorious, unlimited resources, He will give you mighty inner strength through His Holy Spirit. May He grant you, out of the rich treasury of His glory, the Holy Spirit dwelling in your innermost being. I pray that Christ will be more and more at home in your hearts, as you trust in Him. May your roots go down deep into the soil of God's marvelous love. Being deeply rooted in love, may you be founded secure on love, established, firmly grounded and fixed on love.

May you have the power to understand and know the extravagant full dimensions of His love in all of its depth and width and length and height. Reach out and experience the breadth! Test its length! Plumb its depths! Rise to the heights! I want you to know all about God's love, although, it is too wonderful to be, truly, measured.

May you experience the love of Christ, although, it is so great you will never fully understand it. It transcends all knowledge. Then your lives will be filled with all that God is. May you be filled through all your being with all of the fullness of God. May you have the richest measure of the Divine Presence and become a body filled and flooded with God, Himself.

Isaiah 54:10

For though the mountains would depart and disappear and the hills be shaken and removed, My steadfast love and kindness shall not depart from you. My covenant for your peace and welfare and completeness will not be removed, says the Lord, Who has compassion on you.

I will always be merciful to you. My covenant of blessing will never be broken. My compact for your welfare shall stand firm. I won't break My agreement or My promise of love. My faithful love will never leave you. My covenant love will never disappear or come to an end, so promises the Eternal, the Merciful One.

With lasting love, I AM tenderly caring for you.

Scripture Index

Index

WORD Ministries is an interdenominational Christian organization that was founded to disperse the Word of God quickly all over the world. Volunteer laborers have been located who will joyfully disperse the Word. We will distribute Bibles or funds for Bibles through churches, ministries, and individuals.

It is our belief that man does not live by bread alone but by every word that proceeds from the mouth of God. (See Matthew 4:4.) Therefore, it is our aim to feed the true bread of life to those who are hungering for the Word of God.

All donations to WORD Ministries go entirely for Bibles. Any and all other expenses are paid for by special donation, being underwritten by donors who have chosen to do so. No salaries are paid. All who labor in dispensing the Word joyfully donate their time and energy in the service of the King—the Lord Jesus Christ.

To contact the author:

WORD Ministries
P.O. Box 367
Bulverde, TX 78163

(830) 980-3088

The Tree of Life tapestry is rich in symbolism as well as color and design. The gold symbolizes the glory and the splendor of our God. The sun and the moon speak of our awesome creator God. The format of the tapestry is a doorway. Jesus said I AM THE DOOR, I AM THE VINE, I AM THE LIVING WATER. The Tree of Life has roots that form a heart which reminds us of the grace, the mercy and the forgiveness of God. The Tree of Life is full of life with doves and flowers. The roses symbolize the Love of God. The irises symbolize the Holy Trinity – Father, Son and Holy Spirit. The Lilies symbolize the Resurrection. A dove is drinking from the Living Water which flows in four directions symbolizing the Great Commission – Go and take my Word to the four corners of the earth. The pomegranates symbolize the Church and its fruitfulness.

The Tree of Life reminds us of promises in the Word of God – of Life – eternal life, life abundant, prosperous and full of blessing and good fruit – like a tree planted by the water.

Tree of Life tapestry by Becky Patterson